Physical Education Young People with Disabilities

Physical Education for Young People with Disabilities explores a range of methods that will support teachers to be more inclusive in their practice when planning and teaching Physical Education.

Offering many practical ideas to include pupils with specific additional needs across a range of activity areas, such as athletics, dance, gymnastics and swimming, this book will increase practitioners' confidence, enabling them to feel equipped to meet individual needs and include all pupils in their lessons. The range of authors provides a wide perspective and wealth of experience, and all the ideas have been trialled with students and young people, both nationally and internationally.

Written by practitioners for practitioners, this book is a valuable resource for trainee teachers, in-service teachers and practitioners working in a practical or sporting context with young people, and will support Physical Education lessons and physical activity sessions.

Rebecca Foster is a Principal Lecturer in Adapted Physical Education at the University of Worcester, UK, and Course Leader for the MSc Sport (Adapted Sport). In 2018, Rebecca was acknowledged for her inclusive practice for young people and sport by Her Royal Highness Queen Elizabeth II in the New Year's Honours list and received the prestigious Member of the Order of the British Empire (MBE) award.

Lerverne Barber is a Principal Lecturer and Deputy Head of the School of Sport and Exercise Science at the University of Worcester, UK. Her main focus is learning, teaching and the student experience. She has been part of the Physical Education teaching team for more than 15 years, and in 2017 she was awarded the prestigious title of National Teaching Fellow by the Higher Education Academy, in recognition of her excellence in learning and teaching.

Physical Education for Young People with Disabilities

A Handbook of Practical Ideas Created by Practitioners for Practitioners

Edited by Rebecca Foster and Lerverne Barber

LONDON AND NEW YORK

First edition published 2021
by Routledge
2 Park Square, Milton Park, Abingdon, Oxon, OX14 4RN

and by Routledge
52 Vanderbilt Avenue, New York, NY 10017

Routledge is an imprint of the Taylor & Francis Group, an informa business

British Library Cataloguing-in-Publication Data
A catalogue record for this book is available from the British Library

Library of Congress Cataloging-in-Publication Data
Names: Foster, Rebecca (Physical education teacher), editor. |
Barber, Lerverne, editor.
Title: Physical education for young people with disabilities: a handbook of practical ideas created by practitioners for practitioners / edited by Rebecca Foster and Lerverne Barber.
Description: First edition. | Abingdin, Oxon; New York, NY: Routledge, 2021. | Includes bibliographical references and index.
Identifiers: LCCN 2020044282 (print) | LCCN 2020044283 (ebook) |
ISBN 9780367536640 (hardback) | ISBN 9780367536657 (paperback) |
ISBN 9781003082804 (ebook)
Subjects: LCSH: Physical education for children with disabilities—
Handbooks, manuals, etc. | Young people with disabilities—Recreation—
Handbooks, manuals, etc.
Classification: LCC GV445 .P53 2021 (print) | LCC GV445 (ebook) |
DDC 796.04/56083—dc23
LC record available at https://lccn.loc.gov/2020044282
LC ebook record available at https://lccn.loc.gov/2020044283

ISBN: 978-0-367-53664-0 (hbk)
ISBN: 978-0-367-53665-7 (pbk)
ISBN: 978-1-003-08280-4 (ebk)

Typeset in Bembo
by codeMantra

Dedication

This book is dedicated to all our graduates who have adopted the inclusive principles of the 'Worcester Way' and gone on to make a difference in people's lives all over the world.

Contents

6   Swimming   **157**

Kimberley Mortimer, Helen Hope and Rebecca Foster

Contributors

The following members of staff from the School of Sport and Exercise Science at the University of Worcester have written this handbook:

Lerverne Barber is a National Teaching Fellow and a Principal Lecturer of Physical Education. She has taught Physical Education in secondary and primary schools, and has been an Ofsted Inspector and a Physical Education Adviser for three different local education authorities. She is a Senior Fellow of the Higher Education Academy (SFHEA), and her teaching specialisms are dance, gymnastics and learning theory.

Charlotte Beaman-Evans is a Senior Lecturer in Physical Education and a Fellow of the Higher Education Academy (FHEA). She has a vast amount of teaching experience both in secondary schools and in Higher Education. Her specific areas of interest include outdoor adventurous activities and sports coaching.

Karen Broughton is a Senior Lecturer and Course Leader for the BSc (hons) Physical Education and Outdoor Education programme, and a Fellow of the Higher Education Academy (FHEA). Previously she worked for the Youth Sport Trust, where she led on developing Physical Education resources to support primary and secondary teachers. Karen taught Secondary Physical Education for nine years, and her teaching specialisms include gymnastics and hockey.

Rebecca Foster, MBE, is a Principal Lecturer of Physical Education and a Senior Fellow of the Higher Education Academy (SFHEA). She has taught in secondary schools and undertaken roles such as Head of Physical Education. Her teaching specialism is Athletics, and she teaches on all disability modules across a range of programmes. She has developed an MSc in Adapted Sport and is a National trainer for the Youth Sport Trust (Inclusive Physical Education) and Sports Coach UK.

Helen Hope is a Principal Lecturer of Physical Education and a Senior Fellow of the Higher Education Academy (SFHEA). She has extensive experience teaching Physical Education in secondary schools and was Course Leader for the Secondary Physical Education PGCE course at the University. She is a qualified tutor with the Institute of Swimming, and her teaching specialisms include swimming, games, gymnastics and Physical Education values and beliefs.

Polly Lasota is a Senior Lecturer in Physical Education and Coaching Science, and a Fellow of the Higher Education Academy (FHEA). She has worked within the School Sports Partnership system, furthering opportunities for pupils with special educational needs to access high-quality Physical Education and School Sport provision. She specialises in inclusive pedagogic practices and is currently studying for a PhD focussing on the continuous professional development of coaches with disabilities.

Kimberley Mortimer is an Associate Lecturer of Physical Education and Head Coach of Stratford Sharks Swimming club. She has a wealth of experience, with over eight years of teaching Physical Education at secondary schools, including Post 16 qualifications. Her teaching specialism is swimming, for which she is a Level 3 swimming coach with over 17 years of coaching experience.

Richard Pepperell is Course Leader for the BSc (hons) Physical Education programme and a Fellow of the Higher Education Academy (FHEA). He has 15 years of experience in teaching Physical Education and sport in the secondary and further education sectors. He has a real passion for education and sport education, focussing on providing people with the skills and desire to be active and healthy for their entire lives.

Karen Williams is a Senior Lecturer of Physical Education and a Fellow of the Higher Education Academy (FHEA). She has eight years of teaching experience in secondary schools and has expertise in initial teaching training, Newly Qualified Teacher Induction tutoring and delivering teaching and learning enhancement courses. Karen's teaching specialisms include learning theory, 14–19 curriculum and school-based learning.

Introduction

Rebecca Foster and Lerverne Barber

This handbook hopes to offer quick and easy solutions to issues you may encounter in your practical Physical Education (PE) lessons, helping you to become more confident in both your planning and delivery. The aim is to provide you with a wealth of practical ideas that have been tried and tested, which will support you to adapt activities in order to include all young people in your lessons. Although this resource is appropriate for practitioners to use in a range of different settings and contexts, predominantly it has been written to support teachers working in mainstream schools. We recognise that all young people are different and have their own capabilities, strengths and interests. This guide does not promote one size fits all, rather we provide a variety of strategies that may work for some young people, but not necessarily all. The ideas and concepts that are shared have been acquired over years of experience working in primary and secondary schools, mainstream and special, and in Higher Education, supporting students to be inclusive in their own practice.

This handbook builds on the successful publication *The Worcester Way* (Donovan and Fitzgerald 2017), which set out the key principles of inclusive practice underpinning how staff at the University of Worcester work to develop students' understanding of inclusion. Their philosophy is built upon the belief that people with disabilities can be successful in a wide range of sporting contexts and through many and varied physical activities. The book set the scene for 'why' this is important, sharing values and case studies of student successes, whereas this handbook focusses on the 'what' and the 'how'.

Knowing how to include all learners can be a challenge for some practitioners for a variety of different reasons. The authors recognise the pressures on teachers and can see how some aspects of high-quality teaching and learning can become compromised at times, owing to the class size and groupings, for example. However, it is also recognised that teachers still need to be accountable, furthering their own knowledge and personal development when it comes to understanding how to include young people in their lessons. This will include adherence to the Equality Act 2010 and the SEND Code of Practice (Department for Education and Department of Health 2015), finding out about a particular impairment, speaking with the Special Needs Co-ordinator (SENCO) or accessing a pupil's Education Health Care Plan (EHCP). Practitioners who step out of their comfort zone and manage even a small amount of research in order to better support pupils in their lessons are often well rewarded with a sense of satisfaction and professional pride. However, it is acknowledged that sometimes young people with disabilities may not always react the way we would expect, despite our best efforts; hopefully this is approached empathetically as we try to unpick why a young person might create barriers. As teachers, we only see pupils for a portion of their day and cannot always be aware of the other challenges being faced both inside and outside of the school environment. A constant barrage of negativity could certainly change the way one looked at people and interacted with others, so patience is needed. It is difficult to truly understand what challenges a young person may face; however, by using one's professionalism and with persistence, positive strong relationships may be formed between both teacher and student.

Thought timeout

Imagine for a moment how you might feel if you were told you couldn't do something, even before you had attempted it, or being told you couldn't take part because there was no one qualified to watch you. Consider this being the main message you hear when you move around your day. Write down some words to describe your feelings.

A number of practitioners may also be concerned with 'getting things wrong' or in some cases 'causing offence'. These thoughts are perfectly natural and we cannot possibly get it right all the time. When we do make mistakes, it is important to apologise and learn from it. Sometimes the most empowering thing for a young person is for an adult to admit that they don't know it all and that they need the young person's support to find a solution to the issues faced.

Photo 0.1 Creating a positive environment is crucial for inclusive practice

What do you understand about disability?

This is not a test! The experience and interaction you have had with people with disabilities will often frame your philosophy and may influence how you interact with young people with disabilities.

Below are examples of some main models of disability. They are in a simplistic format for ease and speed:

Medical model (Finkelstein 1980)

■ Created by non-disabled people about people with impairments

■ How medicine/medical intervention can 'fix' the person with an impairment

■ How the person with an impairment can 'fit' into society

■ How the person with an impairment owns their impairment so they are labelled 'blind person', 'deaf person' or 'wheelchair user'. This supports the notion of seeing the disability first rather than the person. A more politically correct term would be 'person with a visual impairment' or a 'person who uses a wheelchair'.

Social model (Oliver 1981, 1995, 2013)

■ Created by people with impairments for other people with impairments

■ What society can do to support the individual who is disabled by society rather than their own impairment

■ Recognises that society often creates the barrier for accessibility into society for people with impairments. This action alone renders the person disabled by society rather than their impairment.

Super-crip model (Howe 2011, Martin 2017)

■ Recognises the Paralympic effect on athletes with impairments and how athletes are portrayed by the media as role models

■ Fails to address that not all people with impairments have the same opportunities as each other to participate and go onto international acclaim

■ Provides a potentially inaccurate message that just because someone is disabled and interested in sport doesn't necessarily mean they will be a Paralympian

■ Assumes that if a non-disabled person becomes impaired, they will naturally become a Paralympian.

Human rights model (Stein 2007)

■ Encompasses the values for disability policy that recognises human dignity of a person with a disability

■ Equal rights for all persons, regardless of impairment, that arguably appears to be a birth-right to every non-disabled person

■ Addresses human, political, civil, economic, cultural and social rights.

These basic interpretations of the models of disability help the reader to see which model they may identify with; it may even be a blend of some/all of them. One could argue that there is a place for various models in education; however, teachers simply need to be aware how these models may influence the way they engage with young people in their class. For example, a teacher with a medical model philosophy may feel that it is the SENCO's responsibility to inform them about the specific needs of young people with impairments in their classes. This may not always be forthcoming in a busy school, and the transference of information can be delayed and/or limited. This lack of communication could support the medical model philosophy, where the teacher is unlikely to seek out information for themselves, believing that the young person in the class will be okay to adapt and manage, so the teacher doesn't need to engage in the process. In contrast, that same teacher with a leaning towards the social model of disability would more than likely decide what *they* can do to include the young person in their class, rather than waiting for information that may not always be forthcoming.

We invite teachers to become aware of the various models of disability and consider which model they align themselves with. This handbook has been influenced by all of the models, but with a greater emphasis towards a more social and human rights-based model of disability as its underpinning philosophy. **The young person cannot change their impairment or disability, but we can certainly change or amend our pedagogical approach.**

Photo 0.2 Sharing good practice is vital to improve inclusive environments

Colleagues in the past have asked about specific disabilities that young people may have in their class and what the characteristics are, for example, what are the limitations of such conditions, and what can they expect from a young person with this condition? This approach is based on a medical model view of disability, as colleagues are seeing the disability first. It is very positive that people want to know aspects that surround the young person and their disability; however, there are two ways this information can be used:

1. At face value, the information given can limit teachers' perceptions of the young person and evoke fear of making mistakes and potentially harming the young person.

2. As a guide to pitch the starter activity for the young person, but following this, discuss with the young person their desires and abilities that they want to develop. This relationship and respect can build further, as the teacher and young person find ways to provide challenge and to increase ability in a safe, secure environment.

If option 2 is considered, the teacher moves from a medical model approach (option 1) to the social model approach, displaying that the teacher is seeing the young person rather than their disability first.

Terminology

The language we use and the labels we select to identify different groups of people are significant. Whether we like it or not, people label us, often in relation to the roles we have in society, such as mother, father, teacher, etc. Labels are useful, but sometimes one could argue that they do more harm than good. We are all multidimensional, and in reality, we all have multiple labels, but these labels can also be limiting, meaning judgements are made: for instance, the use of the term 'disabled'. Using the term 'disability' can also be seen as controversial as it means different things to different people. Within this handbook, we use the term 'disabled' rather than 'impairment' as we are using the notion that society has disabled the person: thereby, the person is disabled by society rather than their disability restricting them.

You may also notice the term 'D/deaf' being used within the handbook. Deaf, in terms of this guide, refers to people who have been born Deaf, embrace the full Deaf culture and its community and are likely to use British Sign Language as a main way to communicate, although not exclusively. Deaf, with a small 'd' (*deaf*), refers to people who acquire deafness and may be oral speakers. They don't necessarily feel part of the Deaf community and have very little awareness of Deaf culture. When written as *D/deaf*, it suggests that both aspects of the D/deaf community are being considered.

Photo 0.3 Learning a few simple signs to aid understanding can be valuable to all

Thought timeout

Consider if you were told that next term you had a young person in your PE class that was in a wheelchair, what would your first reaction be? If your reaction is 'great, let me get started', one can assume you have had some previous experience/exposure to young people with disabilities which can be a huge asset. However, if your reaction is that of anxiety, it could be that you are thinking:

■ What will I have to do differently?

■ What am I going to have to do extra?

■ I don't have time to research this!

■ How are they going to do PE?

Once you have met the young person and experienced various ways to modify activities, you may look back and wonder why you felt fear in the first place. It is hoped that trainee teachers who have been exposed to teaching young people with disabilities during their training will have addressed these fears before joining the profession.

In the previous thought timeout, the task was to consider how you would feel if a colleague told you that you had a young person in a wheelchair joining your PE lesson. Consider your reaction again if that same colleague had said 'next term you have a young person in your group that has difficulty walking'. Would your reaction be any different? The Washington Group on Disability Statistics (2009) devised a unique way of overcoming the fear factor. Rather than labelling the young person as the one 'in the wheelchair', they suggest that we re-phrase to 'a young person who has difficulty walking or climbing'. The rationale for this is that the change in the language used evokes an entirely different mindset.

The Washington Group (2009) provides the following examples:

- Visual impairment changes to **young person who may have difficulty seeing, even when wearing glasses**.

- Hearing impairment changes to **young person who may have trouble hearing, even when wearing a hearing aid**. Within this handbook, we also include **young people who may have difficulty being understood** within this interpretation.

- Learning impairment changes to **young person who may have difficulty remembering or concentrating**.

- User of a wheelchair changes to **young person who may have difficulty when walking or climbing stairs**. Within this handbook, we also include **young person who may have difficulty with upper body movement**.

This significant change of terminology could influence how some people may view disability. Therefore, the Washington Group (2009) terminology has been used throughout this handbook.

Key considerations

Some disabilities are more noticeable than others. Consideration needs to be given to those young people who have disabilities that may be hidden: for instance, those with diabetes, epilepsy, or Crohn's disease, to mention a few. Young people may have to leave the teaching area at very short notice, and it may be useful to address this at the beginning of the school year so that they know how and what to do if they need to check blood sugar levels or go somewhere for privacy. Some young people may be very open and responsible in monitoring their own activity levels, and some may desire to take part when, owing to fatigue, they really should not. Therefore you as a teacher need to bear this in mind and work with the young person to find a happy medium where they feel included but remain safe.

Not every young person will want to disclose or discuss their disability with you, which is why you have to make an additional effort to ensure the young person feels at ease. If you are able to create a safe and secure environment, you may find that they gradually begin to trust you. However, despite your very best intentions, the young person may remain closed to you and the relationship may not form as well as you would like. This is their choice and must be respected. Sometimes patience and time is all that is needed, but at other times you may need to assert yourself a little more to try and coax the young person to move out of their comfort zone. If you feel that your best attempts fall by the way side, then perhaps someone else in your team could try. Whatever you do, don't give up; you could be the only one this young person ever opens up to (eventually). You must also consider the fact that a young person may simply not want to discuss their disability with you, as they are completely at ease with themselves and would not want to be singled out. Therefore, always consider discretion and respect how the young person wishes to engage with you and the planned PE activities. Some young people welcome an open and frank discussion and do not mind discussing ways to adapt activities in front of their peers, whilst others will completely shy away from any attention being drawn to them.

One must bear in mind that unless you have a disability, it is very hard to understand or identify what issues a young person may have experienced. They may have a distrust of adults, or they may have a reluctance to believe that you will act in the way you say you will: for instance you may say you will include them in your lessons, but after a while, they may be side lined and/or given something else to do instead. Negative experiences such as these may have an impact on a young person and how they choose to disclose or share information. Equally, they may have had plenty of positive experiences and be willing to share, educate and be vocal in your class, which may well be an asset.

As a teacher, you are in a powerful position and that may intimidate the young person. This alone could prevent them from feeling comfortable with you. There may also be young people who use their disability as a cushion against trying anything new, having been supported and protected that their belief in trying anything new could be a bridge too far.

Please be aware that it is not all about the physical capabilities of the student but also about their social interaction, cognitive engagement, fun and personal challenge within lessons. These can all be stimulated through the activities you deliver, and it is crucial that young people with disabilities are not excluded from these situations. Differences should be celebrated, and some young people are able to contribute in many different ways rather than just physical. For example, problem-solving, creativity, tactical observations, technique improvements, sharing of strategies, etc. can all highlight areas often forgotten in physical lessons, but are just as important for personal development.

Thought timeout

How do you feel when you have been the only one that has missed out on a popular TV programme or not seen the latest film that all your friends have? Everyone else is laughing, chatting, recalling and basically connecting over a common experience. Now imagine being excluded from particular activities or, even worse, being removed from the class because you were deemed as 'not able' or 'needed extra work in another subject'. For you to miss out on key events that take place in lessons that you are not privy to, are lost forever, a connection not made, a social barrier for memories, and potential exclusion from conversations. Despite peers' best efforts to explain what happened in your absence, it is never quite the same. Imagine someone is trying to tell you what happened in that film that you missed audibly, so much content will be missed out and the moment has been lost. Now consider the implications of exclusion from your class and the impact it may have on a young person with disabilities.

There will be young people in your class who are confident, strong and vibrant. You may have a good rapport with these individuals and be able to ask direct questions, knowing that they will respond and feel that their contribution has been heard and valued. Consider what that young person has been exposed to that has made them feel comfortable in your company as their teacher. Relationships build over time, and asking a young person who is not as strong or as resilient a direct question, or indeed modifying an activity without consulting them, could embarrass them. Therefore, it is vital that you are open, including the young person in the decisions you make. Try not to assume you know best all of the time because often we don't.

Consider what the young person can do, not what they can't. Again, every young person is different, some young people will want to perfect their skill, and others will be ready to stop at any given opportunity. This could be down to previous learning experiences and could be a reflection of a previous negative episode, but it is down to you to reinvigorate this young individual to embrace PE on some level. Confidence building is vital if a young person is then going to try something new. Try not to emphasise what they can't do; instead, **build on what they can do.**

Photo 0.4 Using additional homemade equipment can provide a useful stimulus for some young people

We all have a picture in our head of what PE looks like. For some it may look like a competitive full-sided game at the end of the lesson, while for others it may be giggling in their PE lesson when no one can remember the rules. As non-disabled people, we have experienced what PE was like for us, and sometimes as teachers, we regurgitate what we were taught. A consideration would be to recognise that PE could come in many other forms. A PE lesson in a special school may look very different from a mainstream lesson. All young people learn in different ways, have a variety of interests and all need stimulation. Some unorthodox ways of engaging young people in PE could be to transport young people's minds into thinking differently. For instance, rather than doing a target-throwing activity, the teacher can create an imaginary world where the same skill is used to throw all of the fish back into the sea before the tide goes out. The further they throw them, the more chance they have of swimming to safety. Creating a different environment means that young people are still working on fundamental skills, but may improve their enjoyment and give them increased motivation to take part.

Photo 0.5 Creating sensory learning experiences could captivate young people in a different way

How to use this handbook

This handbook has been designed to make information quick and easy to access for the busy teacher. Sections have been created to assist with teaching the PE National Curriculum areas of activity, which are currently games, dance, gymnastics, athletics, outdoor education and swimming. At the end of each section some suggested links have been provided for further information. We are not in a position to vouch for these organisations, but hope that you may find the content useful.

The Inclusive Planning Process (IPP)

Content, consult and communicate, consider, construct, complete and conclude

The Inclusion Spectrum was originally created by Black and Stevenson (2011) and has been used as a framework by teachers and coaches to prompt and guide inclusive practice. Over time, the model has been added to and tweaked, but largely the fundamentals remain the same and include different methods to consider when planning to include young people with disabilities in physical activities. These include Open, Modified, Parallel, Specific and Disability Sport Activity, which are explained in detail below. This handbook has used a version of the Inclusion Spectrum to help teachers, sports coaches and physical activity practitioners navigate their way through different methods that aid inclusive practice.

For many practitioners, the starting point is the activity they must teach. Once the teacher understands the CONTENT to be taught, it is advised that they then CONSULT with others, such as the school's PE coordinator and, if appropriate, the SENCO, before COMMUNICATING and discussing their intentions with the young person. This could provide a valuable opportunity to hear the young person's concerns and aspirations. The teacher should then CONSIDER what aspect of Open, Modified, Parallel, Specific or Disability Sport Activity is most appropriate, in order to include the young person in the selected activity and to ensure successful achievement of the learning outcomes for that lesson or series of lessons (see below for more information). Once this decision has been made, this handbook provides a wealth of ideas to adapt the chosen CONTENT, enabling the teacher to CONSTRUCT suitable learning activities to include the young person. The teacher then COMPLETES the lesson in the format they have planned and CONCLUDES by evaluating and reflecting on how well learning outcomes were met by all young people. It would be worthwhile having a brief conversation with the young person at this stage, but this may not always be possible or needed. If, following evaluation, it is decided that the approach taken was not effective, then the teacher is advised to return to stage 2 of the process – CONSULTATION and COMMUNICATION – and work through the following stages again in order to revise their planning and practice. See The Inclusive Planning Process (IPP) flow diagram on page 12.

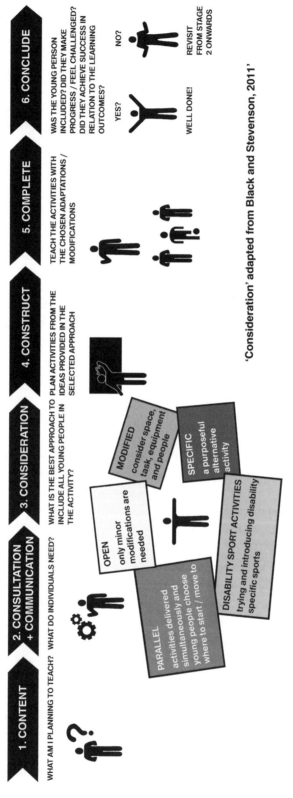

Figure 0.1

What makes pedagogical frameworks come alive is the flexibility and creativity of the teacher. The process could appear somewhat ineffective if other considerations are not addressed, such as their relationship with the young person with disabilities, teacher confidence, teacher attitude and belief about inclusion, their time and the class dynamic.

Consideration: what is the best approach to include all young people in the chosen activity?

Open

This aspect of the model suggests that activities need only minor amendments to be inclusive. Obviously, this is not always appropriate and is dependent on the ability and experience of the young person and the context of the activity/lesson (see 'Key considerations'). Also, many teachers need guidance as to how to make inclusive modifications. Therefore, 'Open' can be considered as an aspiration or longer term goal, which is realised as the teacher develops knowledge, grows in confidence and can plan more readily for minor modifications in order to meet the needs of all learners in their class. Over time, changes and modifications become just another aspect of good practice and high-quality learning and teaching.

Modified

The STEP (Space, Task, Equipment, People) acronym (Haskins 2010) can be applied to help modify all activities by changing the **space** (larger or smaller), adapting the **task** (modification of what is being taught), changing **equipment** to suit the young person (a smaller or larger ball) or altering **people** and/or changing groupings. This is a quick and easy way to modify any activity. The **Modified** aspect can work hand in hand with the other approaches, so whilst you are experimenting with **Parallel** or **Specific** (see below) you can still employ STEP.

Parallel

In this aspect, several skills/drills and/or activities can be delivered simultaneously. The young person can select which skill to work at depending on their ability and comfort. These skills are fluid so all young people can move amongst the range of activities. Each activity should have a similar learning outcome, but the young person has a variety of different entry points into the activities.

Specific

Ideally this would take place alongside a mainstream activity and would be a purposeful and enjoyable activity for the young person. For example, a young person who is not able to play rugby for health and safety reasons could engage in a more appropriate activity next to the class or in a different PE area such as a sports hall. It is important to highlight that not all young people with a disability will be able to participate in every activity, even with the teacher's best attempts to modify. It is the role of the teacher to be creative in providing a meaningful, alternative activity for the young person, with a small peer group, a teaching assistant or a friend. It may be for part or the whole of the lesson **but certainly not every lesson**.

Photo 0.6 When activities have been modified to include the ability of different players

Disability sport activity

This provides an opportunity to showcase the variety of disability sports that lead to a Paralympic pathway. Sports such as goalball, new age kurling, boccia, tabletop games and wheel-chair basketball are just a few examples. However, floorball, parachute games and simulated ex-periences are all worthwhile in developing a young person's awareness of the variety of different sports for young people with disabilities. If possible, avoid one-off tokenistic lessons; ideally a block of work would be more beneficial to embed the variety that disability sport can offer all young people.

There are very few times when we are able to find an 'off-the-shelf' solution to each and every aspect of our teaching. It could be argued that what most teachers need is time: time to plan, time to differentiate, time to talk to children individually, time to praise, time to follow up concerns, etc. The aim of this handbook is to save you some time in terms of both the accessibility of the ideas and the wealth of activities covered. However, your own attitude and approach are crucial to the successful integration for all young people in your class. Therefore, alongside each of the examples used to support young people with identified disabilities in your lessons, it would be highly beneficial if you can:

■ Have a positive 'can do' attitude with all young people in your class.

■ Be approachable.

■ Be flexible and creative with your ideas.

Photo 0.7 Allowing the young person to select how they complete a task, in this example, sending to a target, could be empowering

Photo 0.8 Reverse integration can also be a useful learning tool; in this example ear defenders are used in order to simulate hearing loss in a games-based activity

■ Utilise the ideas the young person may share with you.

■ Include the young person in the decision-making process within an activity.

■ Don't worry if you get it wrong, simply learn from it and move on.

References

Black, K. and Stevenson, P. (2011) *The Inclusion Spectrum*. http://www.sportdevelopment.info/index.php/browse-all-documents/748-the-inclusion-spectrum.

Department for Education/Department of Health (2015) *Special Educational Needs and Disability Code of Practice: 0–25 Years*. https://www.gov.uk/government/publications/send-code-of-practice-0-to-25. Accessed 17.3.2020.

Donovan, M. and Fitzgerald, H. (2017) (Eds.) *The Worcester Way*. Worcester: University of Worcester.

The Equality Act (2010) http://www.legislation.gov.uk/ukpga/2010/15/contents, Accessed 17.03.2020.

Finkelstein, V. (1980) *Attitudes and Disabled People: Issues for Discussion*. New York: World Rehabilitation Fund.

Haskins, D. (2010) *Coaching the Whole Child: Positive Development through Sport*. Leeds: Sports Coach UK/Coachwise.

Howe, P. D. (2011) 'Cyborg and Supercrip: The Paralympics Technology and the (Dis)empowerment of Disabled Athletes', *Sociology*, 45(5), pp. 868–882. doi: 10.1177/0038038511413421.

Martin, J. J. (2017) *Supercrip Identity, Handbook of Disability Sport and Exercise Psychology*. doi: 10.1093/oso/9780190638054.003.0015.

Oliver, M. (1995) *Understanding Disability from Theory to Practice*. Basingstoke, Hampshire: Macmillan Education, Limited.

Oliver, M. (1981) 'A New Model of the Social Work Role in Relation to Disability', in J. Campling (ed.), *The Handicapped Person: A New Perspective for Social Workers*, pp. 19–32, London: RADAR.

Oliver, M. (2013) 'The Social Model of Disability: Thirty Years On', *Disability & Society*, 28(7), pp. 1024–1026. doi: 10.1080/09687599.2013.818773.

Stein, M. A. (2007) 'Disability Human Rights', *California Law Review*, 95(1), pp. 71–121.

Washington Group on Disability Statistics (WG) (2009) Understanding and Interpreting Disability as Measured using the WG Short Set of Questions. https://www.cdc.gov/nchs/data/washington_group/meeting8/interpreting_disability.pdf.

Athletics

Rebecca Foster

This section includes track/running, throws and jumps. Advice has been placed in sections linked to the young person's specific learning needs, but we also recognise that many basic skills, such as running, jumping and throwing, are closely aligned to skills utilised in games; therefore, we hope that teachers may transfer some of the same concepts to other activities where appropriate.

Many skills can be adapted using modified equipment: for example, throwing lighter or easier to grip items, such as shuttlecocks, Wellington boots and pillows. Some young people may enjoy using a dog ball thrower to help fling tennis balls, and once thrown, the throwing implement becomes a handy way to retrieve the ball too! Other dog toys that have ropes and a light rubber weight are also easy for someone to fling from a sideways and/or backwards position.

As with all lessons, pre-planning is essential and often the weather dictates much of what we decide to teach and when. Some young people may lose warmth quicker than others, and others may overheat more rapidly. Reaction time when releasing equipment may also be slower, so allow time for delayed movement. It is suggested that sequenced movements, such as jumping patterns or throwing sequences, should only be developed if the young person has appropriate stability and is happy to progress.

Be mindful of health and safety aspects (as per all lessons) especially when throwing and jumping when the whole class is involved in the activity at once. An alternative approach is to create different activity stations using task cards, for example, 'Nerf Ball throw' as one station, overhead throw with a light medicine ball as another, throwing foam or plastic javelins to improve technique, target throws over various distances using bean bags, etc. With this organised, the teacher can then work with a small group at a time teaching the javelin throw. This may allow young people to refine skills as they rotate around each station, before receiving the technical input from the teacher. The teacher must ensure that they continue to have control over the whole class throughout when using this approach.

Athletics for young people who may have difficulty seeing, even when wearing glasses

Key considerations

This list is in no particular order, nor is it essential to complete each and every time. It provides suggestions of some of the ways in which you can support the young person in your class. Some may be more relevant than others, so select what may work best for you. Safety and safe practice are paramount throughout, and only you know what is appropriate for the young people in your Physical Education (PE) lessons.

Before the lesson

- Where possible, give an indication of what you will be doing before the actual lesson. This can be given in advance, potentially 24 hours, especially if the young person is anxious.

- Ask the young person to contribute to your ideas of inclusion. Empower them.

- Ask the young person if they wish to work with a friend/group for particular activities. Consider doing this discreetly at first if you do not know the young person.

- Ask the young person if they wish for you to share some do's and don'ts to the class about their specific needs. The young person may wish to lead this but allow them the choice. Create an atmosphere where peers feel comfortable to ask questions regarding the young person's particular needs in a positive, considerate way.

- Use of brightly coloured equipment to assist with direction and highlighting obstacles is crucial. Planning of such equipment should be thought of ahead of the lesson to ensure these items are available.

- Allow the young person to have a safe word that can be used by all to protect each other, so the young person can orientate where people are around them. A common word is 'voy', meaning I am close and know you are there but proceed with caution; the word is intended to be repeated over and over to give perspective of where the person is.

- Encourage peers to have consideration of the young person who may have additional needs especially if they can see the young person may be in danger. Specific instructions could be given to one peer to help clarify information given by the teacher to the young person.

- It is valuable to allow all young people to experience working with others outside of their friendship group.

- It is vital to consider the equipment you use for these sports in particular, as missiles are being sent, often at speed! Audible balls are extremely vital and well worth the investment. However, when any audible ball is in flight, noise is often suspended so an alternative approach needs to be considered. A teacher can discuss this with the young person in question and either modify the activity or provide a separate, equally challenging and enjoyable alternative.
- Allow the young person to orientate themselves around the area.

During the lesson

- Consider using brightly coloured bibs and throw down markers that do not blend into the sports hall floor or wall/ceiling.
- Try to indicate directions of throw/movement by placing brightly coloured items for the young person to identify (brightly coloured pieces of card can be placed on walls or secured on rounders posts).
- Encourage peers to 'look out' for the young person if they see them in danger.
- Check with the young person to see if they want to change partners.
- Observe if the young person is challenged enough. Observe if they appear to be isolated and decide how you may wish to address this.
- If there is a teaching assistant assigned to the young person, consider asking for an update of progress.

After the lesson

- Allow the young person to provide feedback on what worked well for them.
- Seek out if the young person felt challenged enough: did their skills improve?
- Personally reflect on the suitability of your lesson.

OPEN – everyone can be included with very little modification

Track/running

- A tether within the warm-up could be used to familiarise the young person to guiding as well as moving with a sighted guide. Ask the young person if they want to hold hands, elbow or shoulder first. Allow time to practice.
- A zone can be created to help allow the young person to move freely. The zone means that no one else will enter that area.
- Use bright coloured throw down spots to mark area (if needed).
- Some young people may wish to use a treadmill in order to walk at speed/run.

Photo 1.1 Using a tether can be a secure way to build up confidence

OPEN (continued)

- There is a teaching assistant card that may help with running in the Teaching Assistant Card section (7).
- Use flashing lights on peer's clothing to help indicate who is where.

Jumps

- Allow time for the young person to explore the area they will be working in.
- Always explain the direction of the run (but start with standing jumps first) and encourage the young person to point to their desired direction of run before they set off.
- As the young person starts the run up to the long jump pit, have a peer directly opposite them (not in the pit) who is calling their name to aid in direction. This skill and distance will need to be built up.

Photo 1.2 Calling their name or clapping can be a useful directional tool

- Tell the young person how high objects are, that they may have to warm up over, for example, cones/small hurdles.
- Encourage the rest of the class to 'watch out' for the young person if they do not hear the commands or they move into a dangerous surrounding.

Throws

- Allow time for the young person to explore the area they will be warming up in.
- Always explain the direction of throw/movement and encourage the young person (and classmates) to point to their desired area of expected release/movement of direction.
- Teach to always direct when young people release and collect equipment if items are thrown.

MODIFIED – Using changes to Space, Task, Equipment, People (STEP) to include all

Track/running

- When running make sure the young person is aware of the direction and length of distance. This can be shown to them by a peer beforehand if necessary.
- Vary the length of the sprint/run. Could stagger starts to provide challenge.
- Consider leaving a lane between each young person (mainly sprinting).
- Could use a young person's voice to keep calling the runner towards the right direction if a guide is not desired.
- Guide runner to be on the inside and slightly ahead of the young person (until the end of the race, where the guide runner drops back behind the runner).

Jumps

- Ask if the young person if they would like to work with someone. Try to vary the people the young person teams up with to enhance social interaction, but you judge this as other young people may prefer to stay with someone they trust/know.
- Consider starting with standing jumps, then three stride, five stride, etc. Encourage another student or teaching assistant to always act as a guide for direction by using their voice, and call their name. Before setting off, encourage the young person to point to the direction they intend to run.
- Ask if you can manoeuvre the young person's body into the right position (use only finger touches); for example, use your hand as a guide to allow them to know how low to bend (long jump) or lean back (high jump).

Throws

- Give the young person the choice of throwing equipment (as this may vary from event to event).
- Consider the positioning of the young person in the class, perhaps at one end if throwing in a line.
- Ask if the young person would like to work with someone.

PARALLEL – activities delivered simultaneously which allow for different starting points

Track/running

- An activity whereby the young person can practise guide running – use a smooth rope/ piece of washing line to simulate unsighted running with two people keeping the line taut from one end to another. The young person holds the line in their hand whilst they move along it. Trust and maturity is needed here from all class members.

Photo 1.3 Using a home-made tool can prove to be useful to further inclusion

- Have a technical station where each young person can try and improve their own or other people's running technique. A tablet device could be used to assist with enlarging images or recordings; audio description may also be useful here.
- At whatever parallel stations you create, consider having an information card at that station to assist with teaching points (have someone read out instructions or use Braille or large font if appropriate).

Jumps and throws

- If jumps/throws are taught in command style for safety, then the young person should be able to follow the progressions.
- If it is a jumping or throwing circuit, or aspects of the jump/throw are being broken down, this can be viewed as a parallel activity, as each station will be different and the young person can work alongside peers.
- Potentially offer peers a reciprocal card to assist in the young person's skill development if teacher is away from the group.

SPECIFIC – purposeful related activity to develop or enhance a skill

Track/running

- There should be no real need to segregate unless guide running is being practised.

Jumps and throws

- If the young person has not been grasping the concept of jumps or throws, the teaching assistant can work alongside the young person using the teaching assistant card. Teaching assistant cards have been created to help with throwing activities (3, 4) and jumping activities (5, 6).
- The young person can throw at targets for accuracy rather than distance or vice versa.
- If working in pairs, ask the teaching assistant to use their voice for the thrower to gauge distance or accuracy. Of course, use suitable implements to throw.

DISABILITY – introducing disability-specific sports

Reverse integration

Track/running

■ By using simulation spectacles (these can be made), allow the young person to try walking, skipping and jogging with a sighted guide.

Photo 1.4 Making simulated spectacles can be useful to challenge some sighted young people

■ Ask the young person to go around a designated route. See how quickly they can complete it.
■ Using a smooth rope or washing line, with two people holding either end so that it is taut, have an unsighted pupil who walks/runs alongside it as a guide. Trust and maturity is needed here from all class members.

Jumps and throws

■ Simulate sight loss by using adapted glasses to hinder vision. This may allow the young person to appreciate the complexities of gauging distance, accuracy and trust.
■ Encourage a dialogue between sighted and the young person who is visually impaired, in order to swap ideas and tactics to help each other with technique or reach a certain target.
■ Have one visual guide who leads a small group around particular distances or targets; they must work together to reach the distance in a set number of collective jumps or a set number of throws.

Additional resources

■ Promote the website https://britishblindsport.org.uk/ for elite pathways as well as advice on making mainstream clubs more aware of support for young people who have difficulty seeing even when wearing glasses.

Athletics for young people who may have hearing difficulty, even when using a hearing aid. This can also incorporate linguistic difficulties

Key considerations

This list is in no particular order, nor is it essential to complete each and every time. It provides suggestions of **some** of the ways in which you can support the young person in your class. Some may be more relevant than others, so select what may work best for you. Safety and safe practice are paramount throughout, and only you know what is appropriate for the young people in your PE lessons.

Before the lesson

■ Where possible, give an indication of what you will be doing before the actual lesson. This can be given in advance, potentially 24 hours, especially if the young person is anxious.

■ Ask the young person to contribute to your ideas of inclusion. Empower them.

■ Ask the young person if they wish to work with a friend/group for particular activities. Consider doing this discreetly at first if you do not know the young person.

■ Ask the young person if they wish for you to share some do's and don'ts to the class about D/deaf awareness. The young person may wish to lead this but allow them the choice. Create an atmosphere where the class feel comfortable to ask questions about D/deaf awareness in a positive, considerate way.

■ Encourage peers to work in consideration of the young person who may have additional needs especially if they can see the young person may be in danger. Specific instructions could be given to one peer to help clarify information given by the teacher to the young person.

■ It is valuable to allow all young people to experience working with others outside of their friendship group.

■ Consider teaching some basic signs that the whole class can use.

■ Not every Deaf person knows sign language, not every Deaf person can read lips, not every Deaf person is oral.

Linguistic considerations

■ Where possible, give an indication of what you will be doing before the actual lesson. This can be given in advance, potentially 24 hours, especially if the young person is anxious.

■ The use of Picture Exchange Communication System (PECS) could be valuable here. For instance, where possible, consider having photos or pictures of what you intend to use or require what you want the young person to do and achieve within the lesson. This could be presented in a list so the young person can tick off the items as they go. Microsoft Immersive Reader is useful to create visual documents.

■ Consider giving the young person a copy of the photos/pictures too; this may include emotions so the young person can flick to the items/emotions they wish to express.

During the lesson

■ Use facial expression and hand/body gestures to assist with learning.

■ Demonstrate *everything*!

■ If using lines (follow the leader type activities) allow the young person to be second in the queue so they can follow their peer until they feel comfortable.

■ Use visual commands (hand up to halt play instead of a whistle, wave a bib).

■ Ensure classmates are aware of changes/adaptations and ask them to cooperate when activity is stopped or to help reiterate instructions to the young person.

■ Keep instructions literal.

■ Monitor that the young person is not isolated. Consider what you will do if you spot this, how will you address it?

After the lesson

■ Allow the young person to communicate back to you or peers in a variety of ways; they can draw, write, demonstrate or use translate options if available.

■ Seek out if the young person felt challenged enough, did their skills improve?

■ Personally reflect on the suitability of your lesson.

OPEN – everyone can be included with very little modification

Track/running, jumps and throws

There should be no real need for the young person to have any modifications.
- Simply check understanding of the warm-up/activity by asking open-ended questions.
- Use arm gestures rather than voice to start/end the activity or to initiate throwing/retrieving equipment.
- Make sure the teacher demonstrates what is required.
- Consider teaching safety signs to the whole class in order that they can inform the young person if there is a need to stop instantly.

MODIFIED – Using changes to Space, Task, Equipment, People (STEP) to include all

Track/running

- No real modifications are needed except for starting the race. Could use coloured cones to depict the verbal words and simply use a specific gesture as a starting command.

Photo 1.5 Using visual instructions is crucial to help with understanding of instructions

- If mild hearing loss, make sure you stand closer to the young person in order for them to hear your commands.
- Allow the young person to follow someone if the class are stood in a line.

Jumps

- Be more visual in your demonstrations in order to get high quality from the young person.
- Make good eye contact.
- Potentially use iPad/pen paper to write down key terms (if necessary) to assist with communication.

■ STEP may not be completely necessary as the young person is likely to be able to follow the lesson objectives.

Photo 1.6 Using visual diagrams and demonstrations could help some young people understand unfamiliar concepts

Throws

■ See above but also consider providing some visual aids to enhance understanding of layout of activity/technique of activity.

PARALLEL – activities delivered simultaneously which allow for different starting points

Track/running

■ There should be no real need for parallel activities, but a multi-sport circuit would be appropriate for all pupils and would enable the young person to integrate with peers.

Jumps and throws

■ If jumps are taught in command style for safety, then the young person should be able to follow the progressions. Simply allow the young person to follow a peer straight after instructions are given to monitor understanding.
■ If it is multi-jump/throw circuit, this can be viewed as a parallel activity as each station will be different, and this will enable the young person to work alongside peers.
■ Provide the class reciprocal teaching cards to assist in the young person's skill development. This resource will be beneficial for the whole group.

(Continued)

SPECIFIC – purposeful related activity to develop or enhance a skill

Track/running

■ There should be no real need for specific activities unless particular skills need developing.

Jumps and throws

■ If the young person has not been grasping the concept of jumps/throws, the teaching assistant can work alongside them.

DISABILITY – introducing disability-specific sports

Reverse integration

Track/running

■ Teacher does not use their voice; use gestures rather than words to illustrate high quality. You could produce cards or teach basic sign language if desired.

Jumps and throws

■ Use only gesture and demonstration to organise the class.
■ This can also be done in pairs with the young people trying to manipulate peers into the correct jumping/throwing position, by demonstration and pointing only. Consider carefully what throwing equipment you use.

Additional resources

■ Visit and promote https://ukdeafsport.org.uk/. A young person with hearing difficulty can attend a mainstream athletics clubs, but coaches/staff will have to be Deaf aware. There is a pathway for athletics to the Deaflympics, and there is a particular level of deafness that athletes should have in order to be eligible.

Athletics for young people who may have difficulty remembering or concentrating

Key considerations

This list is in no particular order, nor is it essential to complete each and every time. It provides suggestions of **some** of the ways in which you can support the young person in your class. Some may be more relevant than others, so select what may work best for you. Safety and safe practice are paramount throughout, and only you know what is appropriate for the young people in your PE lessons.

Before the lesson

■ Where possible, give an indication of what you will be doing before the actual lesson. This can be given in advance, potentially 24 hours, especially if the young person is anxious.

■ Ask the young person to contribute to your ideas of inclusion. Empower them.

■ Ask the young person if they wish to work with a friend/group for particular activities. Consider doing this discreetly at first if you do not know the young person.

■ Ask the young person if they wish for you to share some do's and don'ts to the class about their specific needs. The young person may wish to lead this but allow them the choice. Create an atmosphere where others feel comfortable to ask questions in a positive, considerate way.

■ Consider having PECS to assist with equipment and order of the activities that lay ahead and throughout the session if appropriate. Microsoft Immersive Reader and other online tools are useful to translate words into pictures.

■ Encourage peers to work in consideration of the young person who may have additional needs especially if they can see the young person may be in danger. Specific instructions could be given to one peer to help clarify information given by the teacher to the young person.

■ It is valuable to allow all young people to experience working with others outside of their friendship group.

During the lesson

■ Have signs and colours on the wall to help use as reference points for directional sense.

■ Always point out and reinforce the direction they are traveling to.

■ Colour code channels to work within, and match this to equipment if possible.

■ Provide a list of activities that will be experienced and ask the young person to tick them off as they proceed through the lesson.

■ Encourage the young person to ask for clarity if necessary.

■ Allow rest breaks if young person seems anxious.

After the lesson

■ Allow the young person to provide feedback on what worked well for them.

■ Seek out if the young person felt challenged enough, did their understanding improve?

■ Personally reflect on the suitability of your lesson.

(Continued)

Photo 1.7 Using PECS could help some young people process the tasks set within the lesson

OPEN – everyone can be included with very little modification

Track/running

- Keep instructions brief. Keep repeating what you want to enable the young person to achieve.
- Emphasise start and finishing places, and consider marking these out if necessary.
- Allow them to work with a partner if they prefer.

Jumps

- Provide visual demonstrations.
- Encourage others to 'watch out' for the young person if they are in danger.
- Be aware of 'off-task' activities that may restrict the young person's full involvement.
- Check understanding by asking open-ended questions.
- Use flat throw down markers to support placement of feet (if necessary).

Throws

- Explain and check understanding of which way the group/activity may be moving/throwing. Use open-ended questions.
- Show the correct distance to stand in relation to another thrower and to wait for instructions or a signal agreed between you both, and rehearse this in a warm-up activity.
- Put a coloured flag in the direction they will be throwing.
- Use throw down markers to indicate which feet go where, for example, crossover in javelin.
- Allow rest breaks/processing time if applicable.

MODIFIED – Using changes to Space, Task, Equipment, People (STEP) to include all

Track/running

■ You may need to be aware if the young person goes off task and be ready to provide additional challenge or change the activity in another way.
■ If running longer distances, consider having a problem to solve at various stages in order to stimulate the young person.
■ Have a peer to help pace alongside the young person.
■ If running in teams, individuals can run different lengths over a set distance. This could also be a problem-solving activity where the teams identify individual strengths and formulate a plan to cover the distance as quickly as possible.
■ Have a quiet space the young person can retreat to if necessary (but still within the lesson).

Jumps and throws

■ See above but also provide labels or images of the activities. This may help provide a clear focus for that activity.
■ Consider timing of skills/activities within the lesson to allow practise but not too much of the same aspect. Be ready to move on or differentiate, in order to increase the challenge/change the focus.
■ Try to break down instructions. If aspects are not understood, re-phrase, write down, draw or use an iPad to assist in understanding.

PARALLEL – activities delivered simultaneously which allow for different starting points

Track/running, jumps and throws

■ There should be no real need for parallel activities.

SPECIFIC – purposeful related activity to develop or enhance a skill

Track/running

■ There should be no real need for separate activities.

Jumps and throws

■ If the young person is not grasping the concept of jumps and/or throws, the teaching assistant or a peer can work alongside.
■ Use throw down markers to help with foot placements/run–ups, etc.
■ Allow and encourage repetition of activity for consistency and familiarisation of task.
■ The teaching assistant could also make up a story or allocate points in relation to various aspects of the throws/jumps; for example, try to jump far enough to clear the swamp, and gain two points for correct technique, even if the throw/jump isn't very far.

DISABILITY – introducing disability-specific sports

Reverse integration

Jumps

■ Potentially the teacher could overload pupils with instructions and stimuli, and then ask them to follow a task. This may improve appreciation of information processing issues.

DISABILITY (continued)

Additional resources

■ There could be an opportunity to promote mainstream sport as well as impairment specific competitive pathways such as the Special Olympics. Try:
  o https://www.mencap.org.uk/about-us/what-we-do/mencap-sport
  o http://www.uksportsassociation.org/
  o https://www.specialolympics.org/

Athletics for young people who may have difficulty walking or climbing stairs

Key considerations

This list is in no particular order, nor is it essential to complete each and every time. It provides suggestions of *some* of the ways in which you can support the young person in your class. Some may be more relevant than others, so select what may work best for you. Safety and safe practice are paramount throughout, and only you know what is appropriate for the young people in your PE lessons.

Before the lesson

■ Where possible, give an indication of what you will be doing before the actual lesson. This can be given in advance, potentially 24 hours, especially if the young person is anxious.

■ Ask the young person to contribute to your ideas of inclusion. Empower them.

■ Ask the young person if they wish to work with a friend/group for particular activities. Consider doing this discreetly at first if you do not know the young person.

■ Ask the young person if they wish for you to share some do's and don'ts to the class about their specific needs. The young person may wish to lead this but allow them the choice. Create an atmosphere where peers feel comfortable to ask questions about wheelchair or walker etiquette in a positive, considerate way.

■ Encourage peers to work in consideration of the young person who may have additional needs especially if they can see the young person may be in danger. Specific instructions could be given to one peer to help clarify information given by the teacher to the young person.

■ It is valuable to allow all young people to experience working with others outside of their friendship group.

■ Be realistic with the size of the activity area and if terrain is challenging.

■ Consider other surfaces for some activities.

During the lesson

■ Consider, at some point, reverse integration; for example, allow a non-disabled young person to throw from a seated position.

■ If fatigue becomes an issue, allow the young person in a wheelchair/walker to coach or officiate, but this should not always happen, as the young person needs to be integrated.

■ Encourage pupils to adapt rules to enhance enjoyment/improve inclusivity.

■ Encourage the young person to ask for clarity if necessary.

■ Allow rest breaks if the young person seems tired or anxious.

After the lesson

■ Allow the young person to provide feedback on what worked well for them.

■ Seek out if the young person felt challenged enough, did their skills improve?

■ Personally reflect on the suitability of your lesson.

OPEN – everyone can be included with very little modification

Track/running
■ Warm-up routes can still be devised for wheelchairs or a young person using a walker.
■ Section off areas (if appropriate to avoid body clashes until everyone is spatially aware).

Jumps
■ Jumping may not be purposeful for the young person who has difficulty maintaining balance. Unless it is a skill they can use in their day-to-day life, or have a particular desire to try and perform aspects of a jump, an alternative activity may be more suitable, and this can be discussed with the young person.
■ Wheeling over or stepping over small objects can mimic aspects of a jump.
■ A young person who has difficulty walking or climbing and has upper body strength may consider pushing themselves up out of a chair with/without resistance.
■ Consider an activity where the young person can perhaps practise going up and down kerbs or over a variety of different objects that they come across in their day-to-day life.

Throws
■ Make sure the surface is suitable to throw from.
■ If the young person chooses to sit or is in a wheelchair, the chair will need to be anchored so that it doesn't tip during the throwing action.
■ Discuss with the young person the range of movements. Allow the young person to try what they feel comfortable with, and then encourage them to improve upon it.
■ Allow rest breaks if applicable.

(Continued)

Photo 1.8 Throwing a variety of different implements can be fun

MODIFIED – Using changes to Space, Task, Equipment, People (STEP) to include all

Track/running

■ Reduce the distance to be covered (if appropriate).

■ If the young person wishes to try the full distance, allow for extra time.

■ For longer distances, task groups to design a visual trail (in Appendix B) and allow others to do the same. Swap trails and follow (consider the terrain).

■ Consider keeping running distance no further than 200 m for those young people who have short stature.

Jumps

■ Even if the length of jump is small, this could still be very significant for the young person. Modify approach runs if the young person is ambulant. Be mindful of balance, which may be compromised, so assess risk.

■ If the young person is in a wheelchair, allow three/five/eight pushes to simulate a 'run-up', provide a target at the equivalent of a take-off board and then measure the length they are able to propel themselves.

■ This same activity could be done with left- and right-hand pushes (the run-up will not be straight) but will allow different ways of exploring travel and propulsion.

■ If the young person is in a powerchair, discuss the validity and need of this activity. If it is deemed of no value, then consider creating a circuit that the young person has to navigate their way around and time it. Increase challenge each time.

■ Rather than trying to jump over things, reaching up/out could be an alternative.

■ Allow different young people to work together and offer teaching points to each other.

Throws

■ Ask if seated throws would be more suitable if balance is an issue or provide a static item to rest/balance against.

■ Provide targets to throw towards if distance is difficult.

■ Try a variety of different and 'interesting' implements to throw/fling/push or pull, such as a Wellington boot and pillow.

■ Consider items that can be rolled down a ramp onto various surfaces towards different types of targets. Vary the angles and heights of the targets. Overhead throws/flings can also be encouraged.

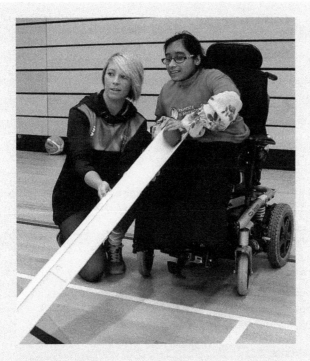

Photo 1.9 Throwing or 'sending' towards a target can be interpreted in many different ways

■ Two-handed throws can be allowed.
■ If appropriate, allow the exploration of different body parts to propel an item.
■ Allow peers to work with the young person to provide social interaction and challenge/ advice in improving technique.

Track/running

■ Consider joining traditional running drills with the examples in the SPECIFIC section. A mainstream activity can run alongside the separate so social interaction can still take place.

Jumps

■ Use a variety of different items to step/stride over or steer around. Throw down markers could be used to indicate where feet should be placed when practising floor patterns.
■ Introduce an iPad station where the young person can video themselves and analyse technique.
■ A balancing activity may be purposeful and allow the young person to practise crossing the midline of the body (left-hand into right-hand domain and vice versa).

Throws

■ See above but consider the terrain and planning of rotations around activities.
■ If terrain is poor, move activities around the young person instead.
■ Have task cards at multiple throw stations that allow the young person to see the Paralympic version of throwing and provide a static chair for the young person to throw from if required.

Track/running

■ Teaching assistant resource cards have been created to help with alternative track events that may also be used as a separate activity (8, 9, 10, 11, 12).

Jumps

■ See the 'Open' section.

Throws

■ Allow and encourage repetition of activity for consistency and familiarisation of task.
■ Teaching assistant cards have been created to help with this section (1, 2).

Reverse integration

■ Have task cards at multiple throw stations that allow the young people to see the Paralympic version of throwing.
■ Provide a static chair for young people to throw from.

Additional resources

■ Raise awareness of national governing bodies (WheelPower, Cerebral Palsy, Dwarf Sports, etc.) and consider local or regional development groups.
■ https://www.wheelpower.org.uk/ includes powerchair activities.
■ http://www.cpsport.org/ includes framed activities
■ https://www.dsauk.org/
■ Also look at mainstream national governing bodies as some do have disability strands.
■ Developmental coordination disorder (dyspraxia) has an informative website: http://elearning. canchild.ca/dcd_workshop/sports.html.

Athletics for young people who may have difficulty with upper body movement or control

Key considerations

This list is in no particular order, nor is it essential to complete each and every time. It provides suggestions of *some* of the ways you can support the young person in your class. Some may be more relevant than others, so select what may work best for you. Safety and safe practice are paramount throughout, and only you know what is appropriate for the young people in your PE lessons.

Before the lesson

- Where possible, give an indication of what you will be doing before the actual lesson. This can be given in advance, potentially 24 hours, especially if the young person is anxious.

- Ask the young person to contribute to your ideas of inclusion. Empower them.

- Ask the young person if they wish to work with a friend/group for particular activities. Consider doing this discreetly at first if you do not know the young person.

- Ask the young person if they wish for you to share some do's and don'ts to the class about the young person's specific needs. The young person may wish to lead this but allow them the choice. Create an atmosphere where the class feel comfortable to ask questions in a positive, considerate way.

- Consider the activities being taught on the curriculum are there any better, more inclusive activities that could be trialled or included.

- Encourage peers to work in consideration of the young person who may have additional needs especially if they can see the young person may be in danger. Specific instructions could be given to one peer to help clarify information given by the teacher to the young person.

- It is valuable to allow all young people to experience working with others outside of their friendship group.

During the lesson

- Be mindful of balance.

- Check in with the young person on their engagement/preference.

- Other body parts may be used instead (if appropriate).

- Encourage the young person to ask for clarity if necessary.

- Allow rest breaks if the young person seems anxious.

- Make sure the young person is being challenged in the activity you have set.

After the lesson

- Allow the young person to provide feedback on what worked well for them.

- Seek out if the young person felt challenged enough, did their skills improve?

- Personally reflect on the suitability of your lesson.

OPEN – everyone can be included with very little modification

Track/running and jumping

■ Balance may be compromised, so allow time to practise if necessary.

Throwing

■ Allow the propulsion of an implement with an alternative body part.

MODIFIED – Using changes to Space, Task, Equipment, People (STEP) to include all

Track/running and jumping

■ There should be no real need for different activities.
■ Relay could be modified so that the takeover box is more precise, so as not to allow advantage.
■ Standing start as opposed to sprint/three-point balance.

Throwing

■ Although a 'traditional' throw may not be possible, an adapted one using a different body part can still project distance, technique and accuracy.
■ Using alternative throwing implements may also be more inclusive rather than traditional athletics equipment.

PARALLEL – activities delivered simultaneously which allow for different starting points

Track/running and jumping

■ There should be no real need for parallel unless developing a particular skill.

Throwing

■ Allow the young person to try the events if they wish, and explore what they can do, rather than what they cannot. Discuss this with the young person in advance of the session.
■ If the young person does not want/is unable to participate, then encourage a way to propel items from a static or hanging position, such as knocking off items from pillars, to encourage a wider range of movement and develop core strength.

SPECIFIC – purposeful related activity to develop or enhance a skill

See the PARALLEL section above.

DISABILITY – introducing disability-specific sports

See previous sections for further opportunities.

2 Dance

Lerverne Barber

Dance offers young people the opportunity to be creative, to explore and demonstrate feelings and emotions, and to develop their appreciation of skills through a focus on the artistic nature of movements. In this way, the physical experience is quite different from other Physical Education (PE) activity areas, meaning that it may offer a broader range of opportunities for the young people in your classes with specific needs. Dance can enable young people to access information in a different way, and it can also be used to support the delivery of other curriculum areas, such as science and history for example. Therefore, some young people may find that dance allows them to explore ideas and access learning in a way that other activities cannot. This handbook does not intend to provide you with different dance ideas or accompanying music; there are many other resources available to support you with this. However, it will suggest adaptations that you can consider within the three strands of **Performing** dance, **Composing** dance and **Appreciating** dance.

Dance strand	Which simply means...	Young people will be...
Performing	**Dancing** – performing actions and patterns of movements in relation to a chosen theme/focus	■ **Improvising** – letting their bodies move freely in response to sounds, accompaniment and music ■ **Moving** – in time to different rhythms. ■ **Repeating movements and phrases** or patterns of movements ■ **Coordinating and controlling** their bodies in different ways ■ **Linking movements together** to create sequences ■ **Remembering movements and patterns** of movements ■ **Improving and refining movements** and rehearsing sequences

(Continued)

Dance strand	Which simply means...	Young people will be...
Composing	**Creating** or building dances, their own and others	■ **Exploring and experimenting** with different movements ■ **Making decisions** in order to link movements to create dance phrases and sequences ■ **Selecting appropriate movements** to express the mood/feeling of the dance ■ **Choosing different spatial elements, relationships and dynamic qualities** to link to the focus of the dance in order to convey the intended idea/theme/mood
Appreciating and/or Evaluating	**Looking at dances**, their own and others, and making decisions about how to improve the dance work	■ **Observing** themselves, other young people and professional dancers dancing ■ **Describing and interpreting** the movements used to communicate the idea/mood/feeling in relation to the theme of the dance ■ **Evaluating the effectiveness of different spatial elements, relationships and dynamic qualities** used to express the intended idea/theme/mood of the dance ■ **Sharing their ideas of ways to improve the sequences observed** in order to develop the work further, for example, ways to improve the performance and/or ways to communicate the ideas more effectively

These strands are likely to be part of every lesson, but with a greater emphasis on one or more depending on the theme or the point within a unit of work. For example, towards the end of a unit of work on a specific theme, there may be less focus on movement composition and more time spent on performing and appreciating/evaluating their own and others' work. You may also have young people who would benefit from focussing on a specific strand at certain times depending on their needs.

Photo 2.1 (a, b) Opportunities to perform are an important part of dance for all young people

What is a dance stimulus?

It is the means of conveying the dance idea to the young people in your dance lessons. It is usually the **starting point** to a lesson and/or unit of work and is key to stimulating ideas from which dances can then be created. Stimuli might include the following:

Auditory cues	e.g. stories, words, poetry, sounds, music, etc.
Visual cues	e.g. pictures, video, looking at something such as a snowstorm, etc.
Kinaesthetic cues	e.g. items that can be touched, things that can be experienced such as moods and feelings, etc.

1. When thinking about **WHAT** to perform, you need to help young people explore a range of different movements in relation to the dance idea being communicated. These can be divided into the following five categories:

Movement categories	Examples of movements in each category
Travelling	Using different body parts to move in the space (e.g. running, skipping, creeping, sliding)
Turning	Using different body parts to rotate around (e.g. spinning, rolling, twirling) and different degrees of rotation (e.g. half turn, full turn) using various body shapes whilst turning
Jumping	Different ways to take off and land safely, demonstrating various body shapes whilst in flight
Gesture	Moving different body parts without transferring weight (e.g. stamp, punch, reach, lean, wave)
Stillness	Holding the body in various positions/shapes, using various body parts to support the body

Most compositions or dance sequences will contain all five categories of movement. However, the choice of movements will depend on the theme/focus of the dance and the ability of the young person. For example, the turning movements selected to demonstrate the swirling leaves in Autumn may need to focus on upper body rotations for a young person who has less movement of the lower limbs. However, by giving young people the opportunity to explore movements for themselves in response to a specific stimulus, they may find alternative actions to effectively express the dance theme and convey the appropriate mood of the piece.

Photo 2.2 Gestures might be more accessible than travelling actions for some young people

2. **When thinking about HOW to** perform dance sequences, young people will explore different movements in relation to the theme and the stimulus used to introduce the dance idea. They will then select the most appropriate movements and find ways to link these together to create interesting compositions that relate to the dance focus.

Decisions about **HOW** to perform will include the follow considerations:	
The use of speed	■ Should the movements be performed slowly or quickly? ■ Should there be changes of speed throughout? ■ Should there be acceleration of speed as the sequence progresses? ■ Should there be sudden movements?
The use of flow	■ Should the movements be free and relaxed? ■ Should the movements be cautious? ■ Should the movements be controlled? ■ Should the movements include a combination of the above?
The use of weight	■ Should the movements be strong and powerful? ■ Should the movements be light and delicate? ■ Should the movements be heavy and loud?

As the teacher, you can use the questions above to help the young people think about **WHAT** movements to use and **HOW** they are going to perform them in order to express their dance ideas in relation to the chosen theme. You also need to help them to think about **WHERE** to perform the movements, for example, low to the ground, use of direction such as forwards and backwards and different pathways such as straight, curved and zigzag. Finally, young people need to think about **WHO** they are dancing with, for example, solo, with a partner, in a group, using a prop, etc.

Photo 2.3 Using different levels may enable some young people to participate more fully in the theme and may also enhance the overall dance composition

The information below focusses mainly on **performing skills.** The '**Key considerations**' section covers other aspects of dance as outlined above, such as how to introduce the dance idea using an appropriate dance stimulus, and also strategies to support young people in the aspects of composing and appreciating/evaluating dance.

Dance for young people who may have difficulty seeing, even when wearing glasses

Dance is considered to be a strongly visual activity; however, it can be experienced through touch and the expression of feelings. It can provide a multisensory experience for a young person who has trouble seeing even when wearing glasses and could give them a sense of freedom that they are unable to experience in many other contexts.

Key considerations

This list is in no particular order, nor is it essential to complete each and every time. It provides suggestions of *some* of the ways in which you can support the young person in your class. Some may be more relevant than others, so select what may work best for you. Safety and safe practice are paramount throughout, and only you know what is appropriate for the young people in your PE lessons.

Before the lesson

- Where possible, give an indication of what you will be doing before the actual lesson. This can be given in advance, potentially 24 hours, especially if the young person is anxious.

- Ask the young person to contribute to your ideas of inclusion. Empower them.

- The level of support required will be dependent on the amount of sight the young person has. Rather than making assumptions, consult with the young person.

- Trust between the teacher, the young person and their peers will be necessary as the young person may be nervous about moving or jumping in the space.

- Allow the young person to orientate themselves in an area, and ask others to be mindful and respectful of this.

- Encourage peers to work in consideration of the young person who may have additional needs especially if they can see the young person may be in danger. Specific instructions could be given to one peer to help clarify information given by the teacher to the young person.

■ It is valuable to allow all young people to experience working with others outside of their friendship group.

■ Ask the young person if they wish for you to share some do's and don'ts to the class about visual awareness. The young person may wish to lead this themselves but allow them the choice. Create an atmosphere where the class feel comfortable to ask questions about visual awareness in a positive, considerate way.

■ Allow the young person to have a safe word that can be used by all to protect each other, so the young person can orientate where people are around them. A common word is 'voy', meaning I am close and know you are there but proceed with caution; the word is intended to be repeated over and over to give perspective of where the person is in the space.

During the lesson

■ Use markers on the floor, for example, tape, to define a safe area for the young person to work in.

■ It may be better if they stand closer to you initially when giving instructions and allow them to place their hands on you to understand the movements better (if appropriate).

■ Try to indicate direction (if necessary) by articulating or using brightly coloured objects.

■ Encourage peers to 'look out' for the young person if they see them in danger.

■ Check with the young person to see if they want to change partners.

■ Observe if the young person is challenged enough. Observe if they appear to be isolated and decide how you may wish to address this.

■ If there is a teaching assistant assigned to the young person, consider asking for an update of progress.

The **dance stimulus** or starting point to introduce the dance idea will need to involve auditory and/or kinaesthetic cues.

■ Pictures can be used with the addition of Braille text, and videos will need to include commentary.

■ If the young person has some sight with the use of adaptations, for example, can see particular colours, this can be included when using images to introduce the dance idea.

■ Being able to feel objects, listen to sounds/music and smell aromas may be particularly helpful and will also support all others in the class to access the dance theme.

(Continued)

When **performing**:

■ Provide clear teaching points and additional descriptions to explain how to perform particular actions.

■ Enable the young person to use touch in order to get a better sense of the shape of a movement or what it means to extend limbs fully for example.

When **composing sequences**:

■ Provide additional feedback – teacher or a peer – in order to ensure that the movements selected are appropriate for the dance idea/focus.

■ Allow more time to compose a sequence for other performers and have a 'buddy' to talk through the movements/sequence as they are performed to ensure that it is an accurate reflection of the young person's intentions.

When **appreciating/evaluating** dance work:

■ Use commentary to describe what/how and where in the space the movements are being performed.

■ Ask peers to narrate what they see in a performance.

■ It may be helpful to 'freeze-frame' the dance at various points and support the young person to move around the dancers in the space, using touch to identify the shapes they are in and where they are in the space in relation to each other. This will help the young person to build up a set of images in their mind of different points within the dance, in order to have a clearer idea of the overall composition.

■ Perform the dance in silence so that the young person can listen to the sounds made on the floor and give feedback regarding the dynamics used, for example, heavy movements or light delicate actions.

■ Allow the young person to describe their own moves if they do not wish to perform.

After the lesson

■ Allow the young person to provide feedback on what worked well for them.

■ Seek out if the young person felt challenged enough: did their cognition improve?

■ Personally reflect on the suitability of your lesson.

All of the suggestions below will be in the context of exploring movements in relation to a specific dance idea/theme, and performing, composing and evaluating dance sequences as outlined.

Photo 2.4 Using a prop or a specific stimulus can increase creativity and enhance performance. For young people who have difficulty seeing, coloured scarfs may also provide visual cues

---

OPEN – everyone can be included with very little modification

Travelling and turning

■ Support shoulder or elbow if needed when moving in the space, hold hands if appropriate, or use a tether if preferred.

■ Section off an area and explain to all that this is a safe movement channel/area for the young person.

■ If there is some sight, place bright colours on the wall to aid directional sense.

■ When exploring different movements, support with additional descriptions/details in order to explain new ideas/actions.

■ Offer to gently move and support the young person through a specific action for the first time, for example, a full turn, so that they get a sense of what it feels like and where their body needs to be in the space.

■ Use tactile floor markings to indicate texture and routes on the floor (this can be created by putting string underneath tape).

Jumping

■ Allow the young person to explore a range of different jumps, progressing from supported, to on the spot, to travelling if appropriate (see points about travelling above).

■ Use coloured markers for young people to move towards, and associate a move with the colour – red could be fiery moves, green could be swaying like grass.

OPEN (continued)

Gesture and stillness

- Use a wall or a prop to aid balance when holding movements.
- Carefully explain the different gestures that might be used to interpret the dance theme.

MODIFIED – Using changes to Space, Task, Equipment, People (STEP) to include all

Travelling and turning

- Use of throw down markers/ropes/floor tape to encourage the development of different pathways when travelling.
- Slowly increase/vary the pace/variety of travelling actions.
- Stay close to the floor to begin with if preferred.
- Could consider incorporating specific props if appropriate in relation to the theme of the dance, to aid with safe moving and improve confidence.
- Include duet work and travel together, for example, leading and following, to offer additional support for the young person.
- Consider adding more or less young people together for group work.
- Be creative with what 'turning' means, using different parts of the body, rather than the whole body if balance is affected.
- Allocate or ask the young person to choose a specific role within the dance, so that they are doing something that is appropriate to their level of confidence but still addressing the task.

Jumping

- Building trust and confidence is important if the young person is to feel safe trying a wider range of jumping activities.
- Static small jumps to begin with and only progressing from this as confidence grows.
- Consider 'spotters' to support the young person as they jump, to support in flight and on landing. This can become part of the dance, rather than it being seen as an additional need.

Gesture and stillness

- Ask the young person if they require a guide for support as balance may be affected.
- Encourage the use of touch to improve understanding, for example, what does a 'flick' gesture feel like.
- Use description to explain different gestures, for example, lifting the shoulders to the ears and then dropping them back down quickly is called a 'shrug'.

PARALLEL – activities delivered simultaneously which allow for different starting points

Travelling, turning, jumping, gesture and stillness

- Using the suggestions in the previous sections above, the young person can choose the most appropriate movements for them in relation to the theme of the dance and therefore should be able to be fully integrated into the lesson with their peers. For example, they may choose to omit jumping ideas from their dance sequences, until they feel more confident with this action. This would not prevent them from successfully achieving the lesson outcomes, as long as they were broad enough to encompass the full range of abilities, which is good practice.

SPECIFIC – purposeful related activity to develop or enhance a skill

Travelling, turning, jumping, gesture and stillness

■ It should not be necessary to have a separate activity, unless the young person has other specific needs (see other sections). All of the suggestions in the previous sections should enable the young person to successfully take part in the same activity as their peers. If a teaching assistant is available, they may, of course, help with some of the previous suggestions, such as providing additional guidance/support at appropriate and according to the needs of the young person.

DISABILITY – introducing disability-specific sports

Reverse integration

■ Allow others in the group to experience partial sight loss by wearing simulated sight loss spectacles; this could be a dance theme, where the class explores dancing with impaired vision. The task could address communication issues and trust.
■ Encourage the sighted young people to constantly describe what they are doing.

Additional resources

■ There are some valuable YouTube resources of visually impaired dance, including professional work. One Dance UK is a useful starting point for further advice and contacts (https://www.onedanceuk.org).
■ Twin Sticks is a concept that can be used to help a person who has trouble seeing even when wearing glasses (https://www.youtube.com/watch?v=wirwGFMp_fY).

Photo 2.5 Using broom handles as part of a 'Twin Sticks' dance is an enjoyable theme for all young people to try

Dance for young people who may have hearing difficulty, even when using a hearing aid. This can also incorporate linguistic difficulties

Key considerations

This list is in no particular order, nor is it essential to complete each and every time. It provides suggestions of *some* of the ways in which you can support the young person in your class. Some may be more relevant than others, so select what may work best for you. Safety and safe practice are paramount throughout, and only you know what is appropriate for the young people in your PE lessons.

Before the lesson

■ Where possible, give an indication of what you will be doing before the actual lesson. This can be given in advance, potentially 24 hours, especially if the young person is anxious.

■ Ask the young person to contribute to your ideas of inclusion. Empower them.

■ Ask the young person if they wish to work with a friend/group for particular activities. Consider doing this discreetly at first if you do not know the young person.

■ Ask the young person if they wish for you to share some do's and don'ts to the class about D/deaf awareness. The young person may wish to lead this themselves but allow them the choice. Create an atmosphere where other young people feel comfortable to ask questions about D/deaf awareness in a positive, considerate way.

■ Consider teaching some basic signs that the whole class can use.

■ Not every Deaf person knows sign language, not every Deaf person can read lips and not every Deaf person is oral.

■ Encourage peers to work in consideration of the young person who may have additional needs especially if they can see the young person may be in danger. Specific instructions could be given to one peer to help clarify information given by the teacher to the young person.

■ It is valuable to allow all young people to experience working with others outside of their friendship group.

■ Depending on the level of hearing the young person has, they may be able to hear sounds/music; however, each young person will hear different things and not necessarily always the strongest bass or loudest sounds. They may sense the bass, certain pitches or instruments. You will need to check this with the young person.

- The young person may also be able to feel vibrations through different objects within the room or by touching the speakers when not dancing. Again, this may need to be explored alongside the young person.

Linguistic

- Where possible, give an indication of what you will be doing before the actual lesson. This can be given in advance, potentially 24 hours, especially if the young person is anxious.

- The use of Picture Exchange Communication System (PECS) could be valuable here. For instance, where possible, consider having photos or pictures of what you intend to use or what you want the young person to do and achieve within the lesson. This could be presented in a list so the young person can tick off the items as they go. Microsoft Immersive Reader is also useful as some words can be translated into pictures.

- Consider giving the young person a copy of the photos/pictures too; this may include emotions so the young person can flick to the items/emotions they wish to express.

During the lesson

- The dance stimulus or starting point to introduce the dance idea will need to involve visual and/or kinaesthetic cues.

- Young people may have found different ways to feel music through sensation from different body parts and environmental factors. Therefore, consideration of the type of music/accompaniment is important.

- When using music, ask the young person to conduct a sound check before the lesson starts; they may want to alter where they stand in the space depending on the type of music being used.

- Help the young person to understand the type of music being used in relation to the theme of the dance, for example, you might explain that you have chosen an African drumming beat for your dance theme of African animals.

- When giving instructions, speak in a clear and regular tone of voice ensuring that the young person can see your face and lips. There is no need to exaggerate your volume or speak too slowly.

- Try to use more visual gestures, body language and facial expressions rather than relying on words to communicate.

(Continued)

■ Think about ways to clap or gesture the tempo of the music to help the young person internalize the speed and tempo. It may also be helpful to tap on the young person's arm or shoulder to demonstrate the rhythm or the beat of the music.

■ Use visual cues for different points in the lesson that all pupils become familiar with and respond to, for example, starting and stopping practise times.

■ Monitor that the young person is not isolated. Consider what you will do if you spot this, how will you address it?

When performing and composing

■ Provide lots of demonstrations, teacher, peers and video examples.

■ Use resource cards to support the instructions provided with images and text (if the young person can read).

When appreciating/evaluating dance work

■ Use task cards to describe what to look for when observing other's work and/or evaluating own performances.

After the lesson

■ Allow the young person to communicate back to you or peers in a variety of ways; they can draw, write, demonstrate or use translate options.

■ Seek out if the young person felt challenged enough: did their cognition improve?

■ Personally reflect on the suitability of your lesson.

Photo 2.6 Being able to copy others is a useful tool for inclusion

OPEN – everyone can be included with very little modification

Travelling, turning, jumping, gesture and stillness
- Allow the pupil to follow a peer if appropriate.
- A mini lesson plan may be useful for the young person to follow throughout the lesson.
- Use clear visual demonstrations by the teacher or on a mobile device so that the young person can access to review the movement if necessary.
- Ensure the class/group is aware of how to attract the attention of the young person.

MODIFIED – Using changes to Space, Task, Equipment, People (STEP) to include all

Travelling, turning, jumping, gesture and stillness
- It should not be necessary for any further modifications, unless the young person has other specific needs (see other sections). All of the suggestions in the previous sections should enable the young person to successfully take part in the same activity as their peers.

DISABILITY – introducing disability-specific sports

Reverse integration
- Teacher to teach the lesson using no voice at all. Allow pupils to talk to each other if need be (or not at all); they cannot communicate with the teacher using their voice, but they have to use gestures or demonstrations or write things down.
- Try to tap out a beat and see if it remains in time with the music you intend to use by turning the sound down.

Additional resources
- Visit and promote https://ukdeafsport.org.uk/.
- Young people who may have trouble hearing even when wearing a hearing aid or have communication difficulties should be welcomed in any community dance group; however, it may be helpful to check if the club is/are Deaf aware.
- Dance of a 1000 hands (all the artists are deaf) (https://www.youtube.com/watch?v=Yk5eCbMzetU).

*** It is not necessary to consider PARALLEL or SPECIFIC activities in relation to this task/activity.*

Dance for young people who may have difficulty remembering or concentrating

Key considerations

This list is in no particular order, nor is it essential to complete each and every time. It provides suggestions of *some* of the ways in which you can support the young person in your class. Some may be more relevant than others, so select what may work best for you. Safety and safe practice are paramount throughout, and only you know what is appropriate for the young people in your PE lessons.

Before the lesson

- Where possible give an indication of what you will be doing before the actual lesson. This can be given in advance, potentially 24 hours before, especially if the young person is anxious.
- Ask the young person to contribute to your ideas of inclusion. Empower them.
- Ask the young person if they wish to work with a friend/group for particular activities. Consider doing this discreetly at first if you do not know the young person.
- Ask the young person if they wish for you to share some do's and don'ts to the class about their specific learning needs. The young person may wish to lead this themselves but allow them the choice. Create an atmosphere where the class feel comfortable to ask questions about the young person's specific learning needs in a positive, considerate way.
- Consider having PECS to assist with equipment and order of activities ahead and throughout the session if appropriate. Microsoft Immersive Reader is also useful to help translate some words into pictures.
- Encourage peers to work in consideration of the young person who may have additional needs especially if they can see the young person may be in danger. Specific instructions could be given to one peer to help clarify information given by the teacher to the young person.
- It is valuable to allow all young people to experience working with others outside of their friendship group.
- Use a 'spinner wheel' or a 'dance dice' with a variety of moves on each side of the dice or at different points of the wheel. For example, the young person flicks an arrow around a circular image of moves and whatever the arrow lands on they have to do first.
- A checklist of what moves they intend to use can be used to help remind the young person.

During the lesson

■ The dance stimulus or starting point to introduce the dance idea may need to involve a range of different cues, sometimes more than one, for example, auditory, visual and/or kinesthetic in order to help process the information. The starting point may also need to be revisited a number of times throughout the lesson to remind the young person.

■ It might also be helpful to let the young person have access to the different stimuli used, for example, a picture and poem.

■ Consideration of the type of music/accompaniment is also important. When using music, ask the young person to listen to it in advance of the lesson, and perhaps give them it to them to play at home; this would be helpful for all learners, so that they could get used to the rhythm, for example, before the lesson.

■ Or use the selected music in the warm-up, so that they become more familiar with it.

■ To aid understanding, explain why you have chosen a particular type of music for the dance theme, for example, a slow, soft lyrical piece for a dance theme about lazy summer days.

■ If the music is too much of a distraction for the young person, try using it intermittently rather than continuously, adjusting the volume, not always having music or choosing percussion/sounds or silence for some dance themes instead.

■ When giving instructions, speak clearly and try not to give too much information at once.

■ Develop clearly established routines with cues for different aspects of the lesson, for example, different coloured scarfs to wave or a specific sound such as a percussion instrument to stop and start an activity.

■ Try to keep the pace of the lesson brisk, but remember to allow additional time for the young person to process the information if appropriate.

■ You could create a glossary of terms and use appropriate terminology frequently when discussing work or creating evaluation resources for pupils to use. This will support all pupils to develop their understanding of dance movement vocabulary and compositional principles when creating dance sequences. This will also support pupils' ability to evaluate and appreciate dance work.

■ Ensure that the challenges created for the young person are achievable, but not too easy.

■ Provide lots of praise and constructive feedback to build self-esteem and self-confidence.

■ Teaching assistants can support the young person to understand and remember the task and maintain focus.

(Continued)

- Provide a list of activities that will be experienced in the lesson, and ask the young person to tick them off as they proceed through the lesson.

- Use the concept of TV characters (Appendix A) that may help young people to visualise how their body can move.

- Encourage the young person to ask for clarity if necessary.

- Allow rest breaks if young person seems anxious.

When performing and composing

- Provide lots of demonstrations, teacher, peers and video examples in order to improve understanding and aid memory.

- Use resource cards to support the instructions provided with images and text (if the young person can read).

- Allow additional time to practise and repeat movements and to remember compositions.

Photo 2.7 Keep information brief and provide demonstrations, with plenty of time for young people to practise

When appreciating/evaluating dance work

- Use very specific criteria of what to look for in the performance when observing other's work and/or evaluating their own performances. This may need to be reinforced in different ways, for example, through demonstration and via individual resource cards.

- Allow time for the young person to reflect on what they have seen and organise their thoughts.

- Use keywords on a whiteboard or a resource sheet to help them formulate appropriate feedback to the performers being evaluated, or in response to a pre-recorded dance piece.

- If appropriate, work with a peer to support the evaluation and feedback process.

After the lesson

■ Allow the young person to feed back on what worked well for them.

■ Seek out if the young person felt challenged enough: did their cognition improve?

■ Personally reflect on the suitability of your lesson.

OPEN – everyone can be included with very little modification

Travelling, turning, jumping, gesture and stillness

■ Use diagrams/photos/films and demonstrations.
■ Give the young person resource cards to use to help aid their memory as they work.
■ Allow someone else in the class to go first, so that the young person can copy their actions.
■ Create a safe working space for the young person and explain this area to peers.
■ Reduce the amount of information provided at any one time, and keep instructions short and concise.
■ Repeat instructions in different ways, for example, not just explaining; ask questions; use a demonstration and find images to support understanding.
■ Reduce the number of movements required in a sequence in order to aid with memory and encourage repetition to improve quality and control.
■ Introduce tasks in small steps and keep a good pace to the lesson; don't spend overly long on one aspect.

MODIFIED – Using changes to Space, Task, Equipment, People (STEP) to include all

Travelling, turning, jumping, gesture and stillness

■ Seek clarity to see if the young person may wish more or less space.
■ Increase challenges slowly as confidence grows, for example, ask the young person to think about ways of linking two movements together, before asking them to complete a whole sequence.
■ Phase in suggestions, adaptations and travelling ideas to avoid overloading the young person.
■ Use camera technology to film work and play it back to help aid memory and focus.
■ Explanations may take longer to be processed, so allow more time if appropriate.
■ Keep instructions short and concise and repeat in different ways.
■ Ask open-ended questions to check understanding of task.
■ Slowly increase/vary the pace of any travelling movements.
■ Use PECS to help aid memory of sequences.
■ Ensure that the young person is comfortable about performing in front of peers before organising any sharing opportunities/evaluation tasks.
■ Allocate, or the young person could choose, a specific role within the dance, so that they are doing something different, which is more appropriate to their level of confidence, but is still addressing the task set.

PARALLEL – activities delivered simultaneously which allow for different starting points

Travelling, turning, jumping, gesture and stillness

■ They may prefer to work in their own specific space within the main teaching space. This could be identified using markers. This may provide added security and give them a little more freedom to work independently if preferred for some lessons.

PARALLEL (continued)

- The young person can choose the most appropriate movements for them in relation to the theme of the dance and therefore should be able to be fully integrated into the lesson with their peers. For example, they may choose to omit a particular movement, or a way of performing a movement from their dance sequences, until they feel more confident with this action/style. This would not prevent them from successfully achieving the lesson outcomes, if they were broad enough to encompass the full range of abilities, which is good practice.
- Allow additional practise time and a friend to help repeat aspects if required.
- Also refer to suggestions in the previous section (Modified).

SPECIFIC – purposeful related activity to develop or enhance a skill

Travelling, turning, jumping, gesture and stillness

- It should not be necessary to have a separate activity, unless the young person has other specific needs (see other sections). All the suggestions in the previous sections should enable the young person to successfully take part in the same activity as their peers.

DISABILITY – introducing disability-specific sports

Reverse integration

- Create an activity where you overload your class with information such as a noise stimulus, inaccurate information and time pressure. This may allow their peers to be aware of anxiety issues when processing information.

Additional resources

- There could be an opportunity for you to promote mainstream sport as well as impairment-specific competitive pathways such as the Special Olympics. Try:
- https://www.mencap.org.uk/about-us/what-we-do/mencap-sport
- http://www.uksportsassociation.org/
- https://www.specialolympics.org/
- https://www.british-gymnastics.org/discover/disability-gymnastics

Photo 2.8 Working in small groups is less stressful for some young people

Dance for young people who may have difficulty walking or climbing stairs

Key considerations

This list is in no particular order, nor is it essential to complete each and every time. It provides suggestions of *some* of the ways in which you can support the young person in your class. Some may be more relevant than others, so select what may work best for you. Safety and safe practice are paramount throughout, and only you know what is appropriate for the young people in your PE lessons.

Before the lesson

■ Where possible, give an indication of what you will be doing before the actual lesson. This can be given in advance, potentially 24 hours, especially if the young person is anxious.

■ Ask the young person to contribute to your ideas of inclusion. Empower them.

■ Ask the young person if they wish to work with a friend/group for particular activities. Consider doing this discreetly at first if you do not know the young person.

■ Ask the young person if they wish for you to share some do's and don'ts to the class about wheelchair etiquette. The young person may wish to lead this themselves but allow them the choice. Create an atmosphere where the class feel comfortable to ask questions about the young person's specific learning needs in a positive, considerate way.

■ Encourage peers to work in consideration of the young person who may have additional needs especially if they can see the young person may be in danger. Specific instructions could be given to one peer to help clarify information given by the teacher to the young person.

■ It is valuable to allow all young people to experience working with others outside of their friendship group.

During the lesson

■ In terms of the starting point to introduce the dance theme or stimulus, there should be no adaptations necessary.

■ Any adaptations needed to support the compositional aspects of the dance lesson will be the same as those described for the different movement aspects below.

■ When composing work for peers, the young person may need additional resources in order to effectively communicate their ideas for movements that they may find difficult to demonstrate themselves. You can support this by enabling young people

(Continued)

to have access to YouTube during the lesson, in order that they can find examples of movements they would like to include in their compositions, but that they may not be able to clearly explain either verbally or through their own demonstrations.

- Build up a bank of online resources for all pupils to access; for example, provide clips of what is meant by dance terms such as canon, unison, extension and repetition.

- If the learning outcomes are broad enough, the young person should be able to answer the task with minimal adaption. For example, if the outcome is **to explore different jumps in relation to the African dance theme**, this may be very difficult for some young people to achieve. However, if the learning outcome is **to explore different ways of travelling in the space in relation to the African dance theme**, then pupils, including those who have difficulty moving, can be encouraged to use a range of different movements to meet this outcome. This means that the young person will be challenged to explore a wider range of movements and to continue to improve the quality of their performance.

- Allow rest breaks if necessary.

After the lesson

- Allow the young person to feed back on what worked well for them.

- Seek out if the young person felt challenged enough: did their cognition improve?

- Personally reflect on the suitability of your lesson.

OPEN – everyone can be included with very little modification

Travelling and turning
- Discuss with the young person what their range of movement is and how they would like to travel, turn, roll, etc. with what body parts.
- Allow the young person to self-propel around the area (if using a wheelchair). Consider left- and right-hand pushing, and reversing; one push turns to create a 360° as a way of travel.
- Create a pattern on the floor for the young person to steer/walk around with various floor patterns to create challenge. Investigate the use of different speeds.
- Discuss how comfortable the young person feels about moving around the area in a variety of different ways. This could still involve using a walker, allowing movement along the floor or being supported by a partner/group as part of the dance theme.
- Encourage using leading with both sides of the body if appropriate.
- Section off an area so that the young person can move freely in and out of their chair if appropriate.
- Encourage variations in speed and pathways within performing turning actions in chair or on foot.
- Use video examples of professional dancers using wheelchairs to stimulate ideas (see link below).

OPEN (continued)

Jumping
■ Discuss with the young person what their range of movement is, how they would like to jump, if at all, and what support they may require if appropriate.
■ If the young person wishes to remain in a supported position, for example, using their chair or walker, consider how they can move other parts of their body in relation to arm/head shapes created through flight.

Gesture and stillness
■ Discuss with the young person what their range of movement is, and how and what body parts they would feel comfortable to use to support their body in stillness or whilst gesturing.
■ Think about using partner/group support if appropriate to the dance theme.
■ Think about different body parts for gestures, for example, if foot tapping is not appropriate.
■ Ask the young person if they will allow peers to touch their chair/walker and potentially use it to balance against during partner/group work.

MODIFIED – Using changes to Space, Task, Equipment, People (STEP) to include all

Travelling, turning, jumping, gesture and stillness
■ It should not be necessary for any further modifications, unless the young person has other specific needs (see other sections). All the suggestions in the previous sections should enable the young person to successfully take part in the same activity as their peers.
■ Although the young person may have a smaller range of travel, focus on challenging them in terms of the control and quality of the movements performed and the creativity with regard to compositional work.

Photo 2.9 Young people demonstrating unison and mirroring as part of a compositional task in pairs

PARALLEL – activities delivered simultaneously which allow for different starting points

Travelling, turning, jumping, gesture and stillness
■ It should not be necessary to have a parallel activity, unless the young person has other specific needs (see other sections). All the suggestions in the previous sections should enable the young person to successfully take part in the same activity as their peers.

SPECIFIC – purposeful related activity to develop or enhance a skill

Travelling, turning, jumping, gesture and stillness

■ It should not be necessary to have a separate activity, unless the young person has other specific needs (see other sections). All the suggestions in the previous sections should enable the young person to successfully take part in the same activity as their peers.

DISABILITY – introducing disability-specific sports

Reverse integration

■ Allow other students in the class to only move on one leg or adapt movements to work at floor level and/or within a limited space to provide an example of difference. Allow them to explore what they think they can do to meet the learning outcome within these constraints.

Additional resources

■ Candoco is a professional dance company of disabled and non-disabled dancers (founded in 1991). Their website has useful information and resources: http://www.candoco.co.uk.

Dance for young people who may have difficulty with upper body movement or control

Key considerations

This list is in no particular order, nor is it essential to complete each and every time. It provides suggestions of *some* of the ways in which you can support the young person in your class. Some may be more relevant than others, so select what may work best for you. Safety and safe practice are paramount throughout, and only you know what is appropriate for the young people in your PE lessons.

Before the lesson

■ Where possible, give an indication of what you will be doing before the actual lesson. This can be given in advance, potentially 24 hours, especially if the young person is anxious.

■ Ask the young person to contribute to your ideas of inclusion. Empower them.

■ Ask the young person if they wish to work with a friend/group for particular activities. Consider doing this discreetly at first if you do not know the young person.

■ Ask the young person if they wish for you to share some do's and don'ts to the class about limb movement. The young person may wish to lead this themselves but allow them the choice. Create an atmosphere where the class feel comfortable to ask questions about the young person's specific learning needs in a positive, considerate way.

■ Encourage peers to work in consideration of the young person who may have additional needs especially if they can see the young person may be in danger. Specific instructions could be given to one peer to help clarify information given by the teacher to the young person.

■ It is valuable to allow all young people to experience working with others outside of their friendship group.

During the lesson

■ In terms of the starting point to introduce the dance theme or stimulus, there should be no adaptations necessary.

■ Any adaptations needed to support the compositional aspects of the dance lesson will be the same as those described for the different movement aspects below.

■ When composing work for peers, the young person may need additional resources in order to effectively communicate their ideas for movements that they may find difficult to demonstrate themselves. You can support this by enabling young people to have access to YouTube before or during the lesson, in order that they can find examples of movements they would like to include in their compositions, but that they may not be able to clearly explain either verbally or through their own demonstrations.

■ Build up a bank of online resources for all pupils to access; for example, provide clips of what is meant by extension, tension, repetition, etc.

■ Create a glossary of terms and use appropriate terminology frequently when discussing work or creating evaluation resources for pupils to use. This will support all pupils to develop their understanding of dance movement vocabulary and compositional principles when creating dance sequences. This will also support pupils' ability to evaluate and appreciate dance work.

■ If the learning outcomes are broad enough, the young person should be able to answer the task with minimal adaption. For example, if the outcome is *to explore different hand gestures within a Bollywood dance theme*, this may be very difficult for some young people to achieve. However, if the learning outcome is *to explore different ways of using the whole body within a Bollywood dance theme*, then all pupils, including those who have difficulty moving, can be encouraged to use a range of different movements to meet this outcome. This means that the young person will still be challenged to explore a wider range of movements and continue to improve the quality of their performance.

■ It is valuable to allow all young people to experience working with others outside of their friendship group.

(Continued)

- Be mindful of balance.
- Check in with the young person on their engagement/preference.
- Other body parts may be used instead (if appropriate).
- Encourage the young person to ask for clarity if necessary.
- Allow rest breaks if the young person seems anxious.
- Make sure the young person is being challenged in the activity you have set.

After the lesson

- Allow the young person to feed back on what worked well for them.
- Seek out if the young person felt challenged enough: did their skills improve?
- Personally reflect on the suitability of your lesson.

OPEN – everyone can be included with very little modification

Travelling and turning

- Discuss with the young person what their range of movement is and how they might adapt movements if required. For example, if balance is impaired, you may decide to restrict some of the turning ideas until confidence and competence improve.
- Use video examples of professional dancers with upper body mobility challenges in order to stimulate ideas (see link below).

Jumping

- Discuss with the young person what their range of movement is, how they would like to jump and what support they may require as they build confidence to take off and land safely.

Gesture and stillness

- Discuss with the young person what their range of movement is, and how and what body parts they would feel comfortable to use to support their body in stillness or whilst gesturing.
- Think about different body parts to support a partner in stillness.
- Encourage the young person to think creatively about the use of different body parts for gestures; for example, if clicking fingers is not appropriate, how could they replicate this move with other body parts, such as foot tapping and head nodding.

MODIFIED – Using changes to Space, Task, Equipment, People (STEP) to include all

Travelling, turning, jumping, gesture and stillness

- It should not be necessary for any further modifications, unless the young person has other specific needs (see other sections). All the suggestions in the previous sections should enable the young person to successfully take part in the same activity as their peers.

DISABILITY – introducing disability-specific sports

Reverse integration

■ Allow other students in the class to compose a sequence without the use of their arms to assess the impact on their balance and coordination. Allow them to explore what they think they can do to meet the learning outcome for a particular lesson within this constraint.

Additional resources

■ Candoco is a professional dance company of disabled and non-disabled dancers (founded in 1991). Their website has useful information and resources: http://www.candoco.co.uk.

** *It is not necessary to consider PARALLEL or SPECIFIC activities in relation to this task/activity.*

3 Games

*Charlotte Beaman-Evans, Karen Broughton,
Rebecca Foster, Polly Lasota, Richard Pepperell
and Karen Williams*

Games play a significant part in the Physical Education (PE) curriculum. Some may argue that including young people with disabilities in games activities is challenging due to the element of competition, the level of skill required to take part and the need for teamwork. A Universal Design for Learning (UDL) approach is suggested when planning lessons from the outset. Employing UDL means that the teacher will consider all young people beforehand, rather than during or after the lesson, ensuring that any concerns are addressed in the planning stages.

Games activities are not just about the physical, but all young people still need to learn about strategy, tactics and working together. Therefore, we can also bring in other aspects of PE through addressing the cognitive, psychomotor and affective learning domains. Cognitive focusses on the challenge of the mind, thinking skills and decision-making. Whilst psychomotor looks specifically at what the body can do. Affective focusses on the social interaction between a team and the socialisation that takes part in discussions and talks on and off the pitch. Adding affective and cognition domains into a lesson could allow more options for the class teacher, enabling them to look beyond just the physical benefits that games activities can bring.

Consideration of how games are to be introduced to young people will also be important. A full 'adult' version of the game may work for some young people, but it certainly won't work for all. Therefore, it is advised that teachers break down the skills and assign strategy and tactical information alongside the activities, providing opportunities for the class to understand **why** they are learning a skill and not just **what** and **how**.

This section has been written generically to allow the transference of skills that are most likely taught through invasion games such as football, hockey, rugby, netball and basketball. However, many sports have elements of throwing, catching, striking or fielding; therefore, ideas in this section will also support the teaching of games such as cricket, tennis and volleyball. Key concepts such as outwitting an opponent will be applicable to most games.

Games for young people who may have difficulty seeing, even when wearing glasses

Key considerations

This list is in no particular order, nor is it essential to complete each and every time. It provides suggestions of **some** of the ways in which you can support the young person in your class. Some may be more relevant than others, so select what may work best for you. Safety and safe practice are paramount throughout, and only you know what is appropriate for the young people in your PE lessons.

Before the lesson

■ Where possible, give an indication of what you will be doing before the actual lesson. This can be given in advance, potentially 24 hours, especially if the young person is anxious.

■ Ask the young person to contribute to your ideas of inclusion. Empower them.

■ Ask the young person if they wish to work with a friend/group for particular activities. Consider doing this discreetly at first if you do not know the young person.

■ Ask the young person if they wish for you to share some do's and don'ts to the class about visual awareness. The young person may wish to lead this but allow them the choice. Create an atmosphere where others in the class feel comfortable to ask questions about the young person's specific learning needs in a positive, considerate way.

■ Brightly coloured equipment to assist with direction and highlighting obstacles is also crucial.

■ Planning of such equipment should be thought of ahead of the lesson to ensure these items are available. Use string securely taped to the ground to create tactile lines to help define areas of play.

■ Allow the young person to have a safe word that can be used by all to protect each other, so the young person can orientate where people are around them. A common word is 'voy', meaning that I am close and know you are there but proceed with caution; the word is intended to be repeated over and over to give perspective of where the person is.

■ Encourage peers to work with consideration of the young person who may have additional needs, particularly if they can see the young person may be in danger. Specific instructions could be given to one peer to help clarify information given by the teacher to the young person.

(Continued)

■ It is valuable to allow all young people to experience working with others outside of their friendship group.

■ It is vital to consider the equipment you use for these sports in particular, as missiles are being sent, often at speed! Audible balls are vital and well worth the investment. However, when any audible ball is in flight, noise is suspended, so an alternative approach needs to be considered. A teacher can discuss this with the young person in question and either modify the activity or provide a separate, equally challenging and enjoyable alternative.

■ Allow the young person to orientate themselves around the area.

During the lesson

■ Consider using brightly coloured bibs and throw down markers that do not blend into the sports hall floor or wall/ceiling or outdoor area.

■ Try to indicate directions of throw/movement by placing brightly coloured items for the young person to identify (brightly coloured pieces of card can be placed on walls or secured on rounder's posts).

■ Encourage peers to 'look out' for the young person if they see them in danger.

■ Check with the young person to see if they want to change partners.

■ Observe if the young person is challenged enough. Observe if they appear to be isolated and decide how you may wish to address this.

■ If there is a teaching assistant assigned to the young person, consider asking for an update of progress.

After the lesson

■ Allow the young person to provide feedback on what worked well for them.

■ Seek out if the young person felt challenged enough.

■ Personally reflect on the suitability of your lesson.

OPEN – everyone can be included with very little modification

■ Consider allowing the young person to orientate themselves around the designated area before the start of the lesson.
■ Avoid competing noise where possible.
■ Allow buddy system or teaching assistant for support. Hold hands, support via shoulder or elbow or use a tether or guide from a nearby position (use of voice will also benefit, or image, symbol).
■ Use a separate area that is designated a 'free zone' that all young people avoid during activity. The area can be at the side of the activity space or within it.

Photo 3.1 Allow young people to develop trust by guiding each other effectively

OPEN (continued)

■ See Resource card C to assist with an activity.
■ Build in time or an activity for the young person to get the 'feel' of equipment, for example, hockey stick, ball and surface control, basketball and the sound it makes as it strikes the floor and speed of rebound.

MODIFIED – Using changes to Space, Task, Equipment, People (STEP) to include all

■ Start the activity slow and controlled and progress at the young person's pace.
■ If possible, consider keeping the class noise to a minimum to aid the sensory development of the young person with visual impairment.
■ Use keywords associated with positions: for example, 'ready' = open body position or ready to receive pass; left or right = directly to the side of them; left forward or right forward = moves slightly diagonally forward, etc.
■ If the audio ball is in flight, make sure the sender shakes the ball rapidly and calls the name of the young person, followed by 'ready?'. Once the young person shouts back 'Yes', the ball is released and 'sending' is shouted. This allows the young person time to prepare to receive the ball. Practise this in order to build trust, starting close and gradually increasing the distance when the young person is comfortable.
■ 'Voy' is a good word to use when approaching the young person so that they know that someone may be getting close to them with a ball at their feet.
■ For safety, initially do these exercises to the side of the main group to reduce noise and allow space to prevent potential clashes between young people.

- Walk the young person out to what is classed as a 'long way', 'medium way' and 'short' distance away, so they know how far they have struck the ball and can get a sense of distance for passes, running and wider territories.
- Allow a modified way to score; for example, have a larger/smaller/different target so as to still provide challenge and skill.
- Overload teams so that success is more achievable in the space provided, or have smaller sided activities so that vision is not obscured by too many players being in one area.
- Encourage the young person to be strategic in tactics of the game; for example, the young person and teaching assistant could draw up a plan based on the fielder's strengths.
- Use bright coloured throw down markers that may be more visible for the young person. Use a brightly coloured ball or bell ball, or tie a carrier bag around the ball to create a noise effect.
- Use a larger, softer ball if the young person requires this support – for instance, a slightly deflated football – or secure a hockey ball to a tether and then to a hockey stick. Or use a balloon or a balloon ball so that it doesn't constantly roll away.

Photo 3.2 Placing a ball in a plastic bag makes it become an audio ball.

- A ball can be placed on a striking tee, so that it is stationary, enabling the young person to make contact more easily with it when developing the skill of striking a ball.
- While playing basketball, consider tying a rope and a hula hoop together and hang the rope over the basketball hoop so the hula hoop dangles downwards, creating a target to throw through.
- Goals or targets can also be stuck to the walls.

PARALLEL – activities delivered simultaneously which allow for different starting points

■ All these suggestions can be broken down further into more basic drills
if required.
■ It may be useful to provide instructional tactile card that have basic teaching points included
for peers to assist the young person with a visual impairment, in order for them to gain high-
quality movements in each of the parallel activities. These can be used on and off court.

Example 1
■ Dribbling (football, basketball, hockey) or running with the ball drill (rugby), potentially
around items on the floor, linear to begin with. Identify a peer to encourage with directional
help (if needed). Also use audible equipment where possible.
■ Can use 'human' cones or tackle bags to provide real-life context for the young person,
Allow young people to be passive to start with, then encourage the young person to move
gradually providing more challenge.

Example 2
Activity 1
■ Dribble and pass. Start by walking, dribble and build up speed or revert back to walking
in order to improve confidence and awareness. Introduce a short pass at the end of the
dribble, and increase speed and distance of pass.
■ Focus on communication and clear instructions throughout.
■ Aim for set targets.
Activity 2
■ Pass and shoot. Young person feeding the ball to shout instructions/directional commands
to indicate the direction of the pass. Build up to dribble and shoot.
■ Routines can be devised to create planning of set plays in small groups.
■ Verbal communication is key and the use of 'voy' if young people are at risk.

Example 3
Activity 1
■ Striking different sized objects off a striking tee. Progress to dropping the ball on the spot
(self-feed). This will be stationary to begin with. Use clear and loud commands to help assist
the young person.
Activity 2
■ Striking objects with a variety of different body parts or different implements to gauge
success level.
Activity 3
■ Directional hitting/striking. Peer to stand in space and ring bell or call name of the young
person who then tries to hit to the ball back towards them (consider the type of ball for
safety reasons).
Activity 4
■ Striking and movement. Rehearse the action of striking, then move in various directions/
locations depending on the game.

Example 4
Activity 1
■ Throwing activity to different targets. Set three peers or use a teaching assistant in different
positions. Use clear voice or noises to allow young person to locate where they need to
throw the ball.

Photo 3.3 Striking tees are useful pieces of equipment that aid inclusion.

PARALLEL (continued)

Activity 2
■ Use a peer or teaching assistant to build confidence of throwing different objects at various distances and speeds. Focus on accuracy. Return object by throwing at a variety of angles or rolling so the young person can retrieve in different ways to practise fielding. Teaching assistant cards may help with this (3, 4).

Example 5
Activity 1
■ Fun progression – integrate the young person into small-sided netball-related game with two end zones. Could begin with walking netball. Refer to resource card B.
■ Net/wall – allow additional bounces if required.

SPECIFIC – purposeful related activity to develop or enhance a skill

■ There may be no real need to segregate unless the young person needs additional support with specialist equipment and to gain familiarity with it, or if skill development needs further work.
■ Separate activity tasks to complete with a teaching assistant or peer that are based on the teacher's learning objectives, for example, the teaching assistant feeding the ball to the young person. The teacher needs to consider these skills in advance and provide relevant detail to teaching assistant. Teaching assistant cards 3 and 4 may be helpful.
■ For items that the young person may have to receive at head height, a discussion will have to take place between the young person and the teacher/peer about safety. If the young person does not wish to receive a pass at head/chest height, then an alternative pass could be used; for example, the young person starts with the ball or the ball has to be placed in their hands and/or the team is given a time delay, or they receive and then the pass must be uncontested.

SPECIFIC (continued)

- Use teaching assistant/peer as a feeder for activities so the movement is controlled. This could improve confidence and allow more practise time for young person before putting into a team environment.
- Build confidence with contact elements of rugby by simple, steady progressions using the teaching assistant or peer.
- Where appropriate, some receiving and passing skills can be developed from receiving a pass on the floor first, sitting down if necessary.
- Teaching assistant cards have been provided to help with throwing for distance and accuracy (3, 4).

DISABILITY – introducing disability-specific sports

- Introduce the concept of visually impaired football both 5 and 7-a-side.
  - https://britishblindsport.org.uk/wp-content/uploads/2018/10/VIFriendlyFootball.pdf
- Pan football
  - http://www.thefa.com/get-involved/player/disability/grassroots-disability-football/pan-disability-football
- 'Hugby' (rugby)
  - https://warriors.co.uk/videos/lets-try-hugby/
- Flyerz hockey
  - http://www.englandhockey.co.uk/page.asp?section=2022&sectionTitle=Flyerz+Hockey+Tools+and+Resources
- Visually impaired rounders
  - https://www.roundersengland.co.uk/play/play-the-game/inclusive-rounders-pilot/
- YouTube clips can be shown to raise awareness of visually impaired games. Make sure audio description is available.
  - VI football – https://www.youtube.com/watch?v=qRDkX_Zv3mY
  - Goalball – https://www.youtube.com/watch?v=lmhL_YzzeFg

Photo 3.4 Goal ball is a game that all can play with various modifications

- o   Indoor bowling – https://www.youtube.com/watch?v=gSNi_xz5yWw
- o   Tennis – https://www.youtube.com/watch?v=WH_sRzgLO6M
- Promote the website https://britishblindsport.org.uk/ which provides advice on elite pathways and makes mainstream clubs more aware of support for young people that have difficulty seeing, even when wearing glasses.

Reverse integration

- Allow sighted students to wear eye shades/simulation spectacles and have a peer to guide them for basic orientation and walking with the ball/stick/bouncing ball/dribble. Bell ball or balls in secured plastic bags can simulate this.
- Where appropriate, these skills can be developed to receiving a pass on the floor first. For simulations, it is suggested that activities are kept at floor level unless the lesson specifically was about receiving a pass at head/chest level from a team member.
- Allow the young person to wear blindfolds and ask them to stand in a circle, then allow them to roll the ball with a bell inside around the circle. This can be developed into smaller groups, then pairs, seated then stood.
- Pass the ball over their heads and then between their legs whilst being blindfolded, they will have to work together as a team and communicate effectively (see Photo 3.5).
- Trust and appreciation of patience is key.
- Try http://goalballuk.com/.

Photo 3.5 Simulated sight loss could improve communication skills

Games for young people who may have hearing difficulty, even when using a hearing aid. This can also incorporate linguistic difficulties

Key considerations

This list is in no particular order, nor is it essential to complete each and every time. It provides suggestions of some of the ways in which you can support the young person in your class. Some may be more relevant than others, so select what may work best for you. Safety and safe practice are paramount throughout, and only you know what is appropriate for the young people in your PE lessons.

Before the lesson

- Where possible, give an indication of what you will be doing before the actual lesson. This can be given in advance, potentially 24 hours, especially if the young person is anxious.

- Ask the young person to contribute to your ideas of inclusion. Empower them.

- Ask the young person if they wish to work with a friend/group for particular activities. Consider doing this discreetly at first if you do not know the young person.

- Ask the young person if they wish for you to share some do's and don'ts to the class about D/deaf awareness. The young person may wish to lead this but allow them the choice. Create an atmosphere where other young people feel comfortable to ask questions about D/deaf awareness in a positive, considerate way.

- Consider teaching some basic signs that the whole class can use.

- Encourage peers to work in consideration of the young person who may have additional needs especially if they can see the young person may be in danger. Specific instructions could be given to one peer to help clarify information given by the teacher to the young person.

- It is valuable to allow all young people to experience working with others outside of their friendship group.

- Not every Deaf person knows sign language, not every Deaf person can read lips and not every Deaf person is oral.

- Be aware of safety if hearing aids/cochlear implants remain in for some activities. Check with the parent/Special Education Needs Coordinator/Education Health Care Plan.

(Continued)

During the lesson

■ Use facial expression and hand/body gestures to assist with learning.

■ Demonstrate everything!

■ If using lines (follow the leader-type activities), allow the young person to be second in the queue so they can follow their peer.

■ Use visual commands; for example, hand up to halt play instead of a whistle or wave a bib.

■ Ensure peers are aware of changes/adaptations and ask them to cooperate when activity is stopped or to help reiterate instructions to the young person.

■ Hearing aids can be temperamental and the battery life span is not always as efficient as they should be so be aware the aids may not always be effective.

■ Wind affects the quality of the hearing aid so consider where you stand when giving instructions; if it is raining, potentially allow the young person to wear a headband or hat to protect the devices.

■ Perspiration also affects the quality of the hearing aids, so some young people may be reluctant to sweat as their hearing may be further compromised; for other young people, they may work past this.

After the lesson

■ Allow the young person to provide feedback on what worked well for them.

■ Seek out if the young person felt challenged enough, did their cognition improve?

■ Personally reflect on the suitability of your lesson.

OPEN – everyone can be included with very little modification

■ Provide imagery/visual instructions and demonstrations that the young person can access throughout the lesson, for example, resource card.

■ Use video clips that have a slow motion or freeze-frame to show further detail and enhance the opportunity to see an activity in sections, rather than as one quick motion.

■ Allow the young person to buddy up with partner. This will allow the instructions to be repeated or verified. See resource card C.

■ Ensure that all peers have a method of communicating with the young person.

■ Make sure the class are aware how to attract the attention of the young person and agree on a sign or gesture.

■ If the young person reads lips, make sure the pupils face them when communicating.

MODIFIED – Using changes to Space, Task, Equipment, People (STEP) to include all

■ There may be no real need for STEP based on the level of impairment. However, the young person may need modifications depending on their ability. Therefore, the teacher should differentiate tasks in the same way that they would for all pupils in the class. For example:

■ Allow the young person to follow a peer rather than lead exercises initially, so that comprehension of the task can be observed before being active in front of the class.

■ Allow the young person to work with peers that they feel comfortable with, encourage them to ask for clarity if they do not understand or provide the instructions repeatedly (if necessary) and/or in a different format, for examples, resource cards.

■ Consideration of the need to give additional time where an attacking or defensive drill is being executed to allow the young person time to familiarise themself with player approaching from behind.

■ Opportunity for team to develop specific signs to communicate tactics and strategies relevant to key 'games' concepts. For example – allow the young person to decide on a sign that they all understand and can use such as 'player on', 'pass' and 'stop'.

PARALLEL – activities delivered simultaneously which allow for different starting points

■ There may be no real need for parallel activities unless the teacher wants to use parallel as a teaching tool for the whole class. Look at previous examples of parallel activities for those young people who may have difficulty seeing, even when wearing glasses section, as the examples will also be applicable.

■ Ensure all activity instructions are given with images rather than lots of text (resource cards are perfect) and support with basic sign language if necessary/appropriate.

SPECIFIC – purposeful related activity to develop or enhance a skill

■ There may be no real need for separate activities of fundamental drills that the teacher would put in place; however, aspects could be developed if necessary with the teaching assistant or a peer on a one-to-one basis.

■ If set plays are being taught and the young person needs someone to interpret or build up the skills, they may prefer to step outside of the main activity to gain this knowledge, but then return to full integration at the first opportunity.

■ Balance may be an issue that can be worked on. This could be done with all young people as a warm-up/skill development section of each lesson.

■ Spatial awareness, e.g. being able to receive an object when the young person may not be expecting it, may have to be worked on in isolation in the first instance.

DISABILITY – introducing disability-specific sports

Reverse integration

■ Use ear defenders to create simulated hearing loss whilst playing a game or taking part in an activity.

■ Add a new rule, for example, no talking allowed during gameplay only gestures, or use a bib as a flag to gain attention.

■ Use flags instead of whistles to referee/umpire.

DISABILITY (continued)

- Encourage team peers to stop play when they hear a whistle and gesture to the young person.
- Encourage pupils to demonstrate or ask questions through use of basic sign or hand gestures (if the young person uses sign language) or communicate using mini whiteboards to write things down.
- Encourage a new word via sign language for each lesson to build and develop knowledge of sign language.
- Get into groups without using their voices.

Additional resources

There could be an opportunity for teachers to promote mainstream sport as well as impairment-specific competitive pathways such as the Deaflympics. Most sports within UK Deaf Sport (https://ukdeafsport.org.uk/) have a competitive pathway, for example, badminton, cricket, golf, football, tennis and rugby (as well as athletics and swimming).

Games for young people who may have difficulty remembering or concentrating

Key considerations

This list is in no particular order, nor is it essential to complete each and every time. It provides suggestions of some of the ways in which you can support the young person in your class. Some may be more relevant than others, so select what may work best for you. Safety and safe practice are paramount throughout, and only you know what is appropriate for the young people in your PE lessons.

Before the lesson

- Where possible, give an indication of what you will be doing before the actual lesson. This can be given in advance, potentially 24 hours, especially if the young person is anxious.

- Ask the young person to contribute to your ideas of inclusion. Empower them.

- Ask the young person if they wish to work with a friend/group for particular activities. Consider doing this discreetly at first if you do not know the young person.

- Ask the young person if they wish for you to share some do's and don'ts to the class about processing information. The young person may wish to lead this but allow them the choice. Create an atmosphere where peers feel comfortable to ask questions to increase awareness of the young person's particular learning needs in a positive, considerate way.

■ Consider having Picture Exchange Communication System (PECS) to assist with equipment and order of activities ahead and throughout the session if appropriate. Microsoft Immersive Reader maybe useful for this as it allows some words to be turned directly into pictures.

■ Depth perception may be compromised, so allow time to process from close to far activities.

■ Daily, functional movements are very useful to rehearse fine and gross motor skills for some young people, so familiar activities over a set number of weeks could work in their favour.

■ Encourage peers to work in consideration of the young person who may have additional needs, particularly if they can see the young person may be in danger. Specific instructions could be given to one peer to help clarify information given by the teacher to the young person.

■ It is valuable to allow all young people to experience working with others outside of their friendship group.

During the lesson

■ Have signs and colours on the wall to help use as reference points for directional sense.

■ Always point out and reinforce the direction they are travelling to.

■ Colour code channels to work within and match this to equipment if possible.

■ Provide a list of activities that will be experienced and ask the young person to tick them off as they proceed through the lesson.

■ Provide a glossary of key terms you may use throughout the lesson.

■ Encourage the young person to ask for clarity if necessary.

■ Allow rest breaks if the young person seems anxious.

■ Reference TV characters (as suggested in Appendix A) that may support the young person in visualising and copying particular actions.

■ Keep explanations simple and be ready to repeat but don't always re-phrase.

■ Encourage turn taking with attempts of activities and patience when waiting for instructions.

■ You can use fixations that the young person may have to motivate and encourage participation.

■ Allow extra practise time.

■ Encourage eye contact.

(Continued)

After the lesson

- Allow the young person to provide feedback on what worked well for them.
- Seek out if the young person felt challenged enough, did their cognition improve?
- Personally reflect on the suitability of your lesson.

OPEN – everyone can be included with very little modification

- Allow teaching assistant/young person to have knowledge of activities prior to the lesson. This may save time during the activity.
- Include imagery and visual demonstrations that can be repeated/accessed throughout the lesson.
- Allow the option for a 'safe or quiet zone' if the young person requires this. Explain this to all young people if needed.
- Break the skill down step by step. Repeat instructions but don't re-phrase. Use diagrams and technology if needed.
- Focus on movement across centre mid line, for example, passing a ball with right foot to partners left foot , etc.
- Try to work in the same environment and avoid change unless the young person is warned in advance.
- Use emoji cards as part of a warm-up to act out emotions/actions. Encourage eye contact.
- Reinforce turn taking if shooting, dribbling, etc.
- See resource card C.

MODIFIED – Using changes to Space, Task, Equipment, People (STEP) to include all

- Build up instructions step by step; consider not overloading choice in the first instance if the activity is new.
- Create a personal activity board so they know what they have to do and what is coming next. Allow them to check items off if necessary.
- Use simple language and repeat clearly. If message is still not understood, have resource cards ready to support specific activities.
- Allow extra time for activity or instructions (if the young person requires).
- Use demonstrations throughout.
- Create a multi-sensory environment to engage senses.
- Consider creating a quiet zone should the young person require a timeout.
- Ask open-ended questions and use written questions or imagery if suitable to the young person. This will identify their level of knowledge and understanding.
- Begin with straight-line dribble and short distance passes. Add in turns and further distance as progressions.
- Keeping to a single line may help the young person maintain focus. Experiment between using right and left feet to keep ball close to the line (football, hockey).
- Allow the young person time to dribble with ball at feet/hand following predetermined line using cones, spot mats or chalk.

- Slow the pace accordingly and allow walking rather than running initially. Try to develop into a jog, etc.
- If necessary, use resource card to assist the young person with high-quality moves, offer demonstrations and repeat instructions.
- Devise a scoring system whereby the young person gains points if they make contact/pass the ball.
- Increase points scored if the young person can dribble and score (progression from static shooting).
- Be realistic in equipment size and fielding/throwing distances to match the ability of the young person.
- If having to keep score is necessary, use a floor marker to help keep a visible indication of their progress.
- Allow the young person to replicate 'dribble' by bouncing the ball with their hands and then throw as a shooting activity (basketball) or can shoot/propel (football).
- Pass the ball to a static feature, for example, a wall. Use a larger ball initially. If the young person can complete five successful passes and control the rebound, they can experiment with a smaller ball.
- Encourage the young person to allow the ball to drop by their foot before making contact.
- Focus on allowing extra time for the young person to react to the movement of the object when striking and fielding. Allow time to repeat demonstrations and explanations. Modify equipment by using a balloon ball.
- Allow the young person a choice of three balls, (small, medium and large). Set a large goal mouth for the young person to score, ensuring success.
- Can use characters from films to assist with the young person's understanding of specific movements (see Appendix A).
- Use a striking tee to develop technique and confidence.
- The young person could attach a strap to their wrist and allow the ball to hang by foot/hand/stick. Once the pass has been made, the ball will only travel as far as the rebound cord will allow.
- Use of padded equipment such as shields or bags to simulate contact when practising tackling, rucking and mauling.
- Use a rebound ball and/or net (cost associated).
- Use the young person as a feeder to get used to the activity.
- Allow a partner or teaching assistant to work with the young person at a slower pace, breaking the activity down.
- Develop set piece skills in isolation with reduced pressure.
- Allow additional bounces to allow the young person to retrieve/send back the item.
- Lower density ball may help.
- Find out what the young person may like (e.g. a preference for the colour green, allow them to have access to the green equipment).
- Find out if the young person has an interest in a particular character from a film/hobby that can be used to distract or bring focus in. For example, a target on the wall could be of their favourite character.

PARALLEL – activities delivered simultaneously which allow for different starting points

- All these suggestions can be broken down further into more basic drills.
- It may be useful to provide instructional cards that have basic teaching points included for peers to assist each other in order for them to gain high-quality movements in each of the parallel activities.

Example 1

Activity 1 (netball, hockey, basketball, rugby)

- Instead of remembering positions and areas, coloured spots or cones could mark out areas for students to remain in throughout the duration of the activity and work within whilst still maintaining elements of the original game. See resource card A.

Activity 2

- Allow game play to be played at a walking pace so that there is more time for decision-making and concentrating on tasks within the game scenario. See resource card B.

Example 2 (striking and fielding)

Activity 1

- Throwing and catching different items at different heights and speeds as appropriate to focus on fielding or defending.

Activity 2

- As above but progress to allocated areas with walking pace getting quicker and with a specific ball/type of throw.

Activity 3

- Striking different sized objects off a striking tee. Progress to dropping the ball on the spot (self-feed). This will be done stationary to begin with.
- Use clear and loud commands to help assist the young person.
- Use of iPads to record demonstrations to help analyse technique.

SPECIFIC – purposeful related activity to develop or enhance a skill

- Refer to the previous SPECIFIC section but focus on developing skill. All activities above can be adjusted to small groups or one on one, to encourage different people working together to improve the particular skill. Remind those working together to:
- Repeat and remind the young person of the instructions throughout.
- Use demonstrations to build confidence and replicate teaching points.
- Use resource cards with teaching assistant to regain focus on task.
- Allow other peers to work with the young person where possible so as to not always segregated from the entire class.

DISABILITY – introducing disability-specific sports

- There are a number of organisations that can raise awareness for all young people and their friends. There could be an opportunity for you to promote mainstream sport as well as impairment-specific competitive pathways such as the Special Olympics. Try:
- https://www.mencap.org.uk/about-us/what-we-do/mencap-sport
- http://www.uksportsassociation.org/
- https://www.specialolympics.org/

DISABILITY (continued)

Reverse integration

- YouTube clips can be shared to show the level of competition and skill. Could try to develop/copy set plays from the clips used.
- Non-contact versions such as tag or touch rugby or adapted 'hugby' can be played (https://warriors.co.uk/videos/lets-try-hugby/).
- Create an environment that over stimulates people, and then ask them to learn a new skill to show the complexities of distractions etc. Try http://boccia.uk.com/ or http://gbkurling.co.uk/.

Games for young people who may have difficulty walking or climbing stairs

Key considerations

This list is in no particular order, nor is it essential to complete each and every time. It provides suggestions of some of the ways in which you can support the young person in your class. Some may be more relevant than others, so select what may work best for you. Safety and safe practice are paramount throughout, and only you know what is appropriate for the young people in your PE lessons.

Before the lesson

- Where possible, give an indication of what you will be doing before the actual lesson. This can be given in advance, potentially 24 hours, especially if the young person is anxious.

- Ask the young person to contribute to your ideas of inclusion. Empower them.

- Ask the young person if they wish to work with a friend/group for particular activities. Consider doing this discreetly at first if you do not know the young person.

- Ask the young person if they wish for you to share some do's and don'ts to the class about wheelchair, walker and movement etiquette. The young person may wish to lead this but allow them the choice. Create an atmosphere where peers feel comfortable to ask questions to increase awareness of the young person's particular needs in a positive, considerate way.

- Encourage peers to work in consideration of the young person who may have additional needs especially if they can see the young person may be in danger. Specific instructions could be given to one peer to help clarify information given by the teacher to the young person.

- It is valuable to allow all young people to experience working with others outside of their friendship group.

(Continued)

During the lesson

■ Allow reverse integration, and allow a peer to be in a wheelchair (if you have access to wheelchairs) to balance out a side in the game (if possible and appropriate). Or play using crutches or a walker if the school has access to them.

■ If fatigue becomes an issue, allow the young person who has difficulty walking to coach or officiate, but this should not always happen as the young person needs to be integrated, so avoid using this method repeatedly.

■ Allow and encourage pupils to adapt rules to enhance enjoyment and inclusivity themselves.

■ Allow a separate 'buffer' zone to prevent or minimise injuries from wheelchair or walker by zoning areas.

■ Be realistic with the size of the activity area as it is most likely the young person who has difficulty walking will need space to turn to try and bring the ball to a standstill.

■ Allow support aids, bolsters or standing platforms, and use of foam gym wedges, banana gym rockers, soft play shape tunnels and Swiss balls to support movement. Also allow partners for support.

■ Encourage the young person to ask for clarity if necessary.

■ Allow rest breaks if the young person seems anxious.

After the lesson

■ Allow the young person to provide feedback on what worked well for them.

■ Seek out if the young person felt challenged enough, did their cognition improve?

■ Personally reflect on the suitability of your lesson.

OPEN – everyone can be included with very little modification

■ Create a separate/safe zone to allow the young person to move freely and to prevent any collision with other young people during the warm-up. When the young person and peers are confident and are spatially aware, allow integration together. Begin this by small progressions, for example, only two people allowed in the 'free zone', then four, etc.

■ Allow the young person to be at the 'centre' position, so people can move towards them and they can remain more stationary if necessary.

■ If the young person has mobility issues, increase activity of arms, and change use of feet to arms to replicate transferable skills. A static activity but with vigorous use of arms (if applicable) could still raise heart rate. Allow rest breaks/timeouts if necessary.

■ If a travelling warm-up is used, provide a range of distances to suit ability and allow choice of how far to travel.

OPEN (continued)

- Break down the movement and allow repetition of action before moving on.
- Repeat demonstrations and instructions (use young people to help integrate each other).
- Where possible, try to build in opposite hand to opposite leg, etc., crossing the centre line of the body to develop coordination.

MODIFIED – Using changes to Space, Task, Equipment, People (STEP) to include all

- Consider the surface where the sport will take place. Is the surface smooth and easy for the young person to travel across without much resistance? If you are timetabled onto the fields, is there a better surface close to the lesson so you can potentially manage two areas?
- Consider the distance of activities in relation to the mobility of the young person. Differentiate distances to travel to and from.
- Allow the young person to 'adjust' and modify distances travelled or 'rules' to suit their ability, ensuring they are comfortable.
- Discuss retrieval of items thrown or sent/propelled. Does the young person collect the object for themselves, or do they require an assistant? Can something be placed at their side so they can retrieve the balls from waist height rather than trying to reach downwards, that is, a chair?

Photo 3.6 Using additional, everyday equipment could support inclusion, for example, using a chair to put equipment on

MODIFIED (continued)

- Focus on technique and skill set before speed/intensity.
- Allow the young person to contribute to the adaptation of the task.
- Adapt the activity to incorporate a wheelchair or support walker, targets or goals near the young person.
- Allow the young person to replicate 'dribble' by bouncing the ball with their hands, and then throw as a shooting activity (basketball), or can use front of the wheelchair /walker to dribble and shoot/propel (football).
- Give the young person different targets to aim for when striking and throwing to focus on crossing the centre line of body to develop coordination.
- Implement small-sided activities to reduce pressure or encourage competition.
- Use a larger ball, which is lighter/softer, allowing the young person more time to react. This will also make it easier for peers to deliver a pass to the young person. Balloons and balloon balls may also be a useful addition to allow reaction time.
- A larger ball will also allow the young person to dribble with their chair or walker. If playing football, a large gym ball could be an alternative for the young person to control/manipulate.

Photo 3.7 Sometimes large gym balls could be used as an alternative if specialist equipment is not available

- If equipment is available, create a game environment/activity with a wheelchair player on each team, such as Inclusive Zone Basketball.
- Start with a ball/bat that may be lighter and slower so it gives the young person time to react.
- A striking tee can be used to assist in striking accuracy.
- Use a rebound ball (cost associated). The young person can attach strap to their wrist and allow the ball to hang by foot/hand/stick.
- A ramp/plastic drainpipe can be used to propel things from a seated position.

MODIFIED (continued)

- Ask if the young person wants an assistant or would prefer someone to push them at times.
- Allow more students on the young person's team to create a competitive environment.
- Ask if the young person wants a 'runner' for some activities.
- Consider encouraging a distance 'kick' if appropriate, from a seated or standing position.
- Allow an extra bounce for net/wall games.
- Net/wall games can be played on a bench or tabletop. Put a cone and rope as a barrier for the net.
- Some tables that are irregular in shape can be put together so there is a hole in the middle. Balls can be thrown onto/off the table and into the hole. This could be done from a seated position; if someone is opposite, they can move to retrieve the ball and send it back to the young person. More people could be around the table creating a team effort of allowing the ball to bounce on the table and sending it back onto the table.

PARALLEL – activities delivered simultaneously which allow for different starting points

- All these suggestions can be broken down further into more basic drills. It may be useful to provide instructional cards that have basic teaching points included for peers to assist each other, in order for them to gain high-quality movements in each of the parallel activities. If necessary, break activities down to stationary, then build up in parallel activities to improve the young person's confidence and ability.

If a parallel lesson is possible, one could offer the following as ideas:

Example 1

Activity 1

- Pass/roll ball to a static feature, for example, a wall. Use a larger ball initially. If the young person can complete five successful passes and control the rebound, they can experiment with a smaller ball. Gradually add more challenge.

Activity 2

- Allow the young person time to dribble with ball at feet/hand/using their wheelchair/walker following a predetermined line (using cones, spot mats or chalk).
- Walking/rolling pace to be encouraged initially. Keeping to a single line may help the young person maintain focus and experiment between using right and left feet to keep the ball close to the line (if appropriate).

Activity 3

- Allow the young person a choice of three balls (small, medium and large). Set a large goal mouth for the young person to score, ensuring success.

Example 2

Activity 1

- Striking different sized objects off a striking tee. Progress onto dropping the ball on the spot (self-feed). This will be done stationary to begin with.

Activity 2

- Throwing activity to different targets. Select three classmates or use teaching assistant in different positions.

Activity 3

- Use buddy system or teaching assistant to build confidence of throwing different objects at different distances and speeds. Focus on accuracy. Return the object by throwing at different angles or rolling so that the young person can retrieve in different ways to practise fielding.

PARALLEL (continued)

- Multi-activity stations would be ideal for young people with developmental coordination difficulties where they can practise a skill over and over to rehearse the movement, then move on; these activities work on agility, balance, space perception, speed, accuracy and coordination. The same activities over a six- to eight-week period could help with fine and gross motor skills, such as throw and catch a light scarf, throw and catch a large ball, sending to one hand and then move to catch with other, and pulling themselves on their tummies down a bench.
- Number spots – young people have to run/walk to touch random numbered spots on the floor in whatever order is given.
- Swamp crossing – using only two spots the young person has to move across a set distance to stand on.
- Crossover – there will be two hoops on floor: five red bean bags placed in blue hoop, and five blue bean bags in red hoop. The young person is in the middle of hoops and has to move sideways to pick up opposing coloured bean bag and cross across the body (midline) to release using other hand into other hoop.
- Target throw – throw bean bags into three hoops placed on floor, various distances apart.
- Dribble a ball – using feet or hands (bouncing) dribble a ball through cones and/or square.
- Throw against a wall – throw and catch against a wall.
- Agility circuit – add aspects of above into a circuit that the young person can be timed doing.

SPECIFIC – purposeful related activity to develop or enhance a skill

- Select an appropriate area for the young person, for example, the school playground. Using chalk, draw channels for the young person to practise dribbling. Ideally the young person should work as close to the group as possible. The locations and these activities need to be close enough in order that the teacher can supervise both groups.
- Challenge the young person by decreasing the width of channel, using different size balls, and vary the striking implements.
- Develop activities whereby the young person tries to stop items being rolled to them.
- With a partner (teaching assistant may be more appropriate initially), stand 1-meter apart placing hands on each other's shoulders. This should form a solid triangular base, creating a 'human walker'. The aim of the game is to keep the ball between each other by passing it backwards and forwards. Once confident in using each other for support, encourage walking with the ball (ensure initially that the young person with lower body impairment is the one in the partnership that is walking forwards and the partner will be walking backwards).
- If the young person feels confident and competent to do so, they can try changing direction, still maintaining control of the ball. Once confidence and competence improve, provide a new challenge.
- Teaching assistant cards have been created to help with accuracy and distance (1, 2).

DISABILITY – introducing disability-specific sports

- If the organisation has access to multiple wheelchairs, the class could be involved in wheelchair-based activities. Small-sided team games of basketball and rugby are useful. If only one or two chairs are available, then adapt to 'Inclusive Zone' activities. If the young person is the only person in the class who has access to a wheelchair, consider seated volleyball and seated hockey and play adapted versions of these games. These games could be used as parallel or separate activities.
- Raise awareness of national governing bodies (WheelPower, Cerebral Palsy, Dwarf Sports, etc.) and consider local or regional development groups (Powerchair football or frame football).
  - o https://www.wheelpower.org.uk/ includes powerchair activities
  - o http://www.cpsport.org/ includes framed activities
  - o https://www.dsauk.org/ access to events –
- Also look at mainstream National Governing Bodies as some do have disability strands. Developmental Co-ordination Disorder (dyspraxia) has an informative website http://elearning.canchild.ca/dcd_workshop/sports.html, including http://limbpower.com/.
- Consider wheelchair cricket: https://www.ukwheelchaircricket.com/.

Photo 3.8 Wheelchair cricket is another exciting inclusive game that all can play

Reverse integration

- If the organisation has wheelchairs, the whole class will take part in the activities using wheelchairs whilst exploring:
  - o Fundamental rolling skills, starting, stopping and changing direction.
  - o Throwing, catching and sending from stationary and then with movement.
  - o Team sports such as wheelchair basketball or wheelchair rugby.
- If organisation does not have wheelchairs, try exploring.
  - o Use static everyday chairs to do tasks such as throw, catch, transfer items and aiming.
  - o Use a seated hockey channel with benches on their side.
  - o Sportability adapted tabletop games, such as tabletop cricket, polybat, table tennis, blow football, Subbuteo and 'life-sized' table cricket (see photo below).
- Allow other team to have a seated player, for example, bowler.
- Consider introducing the game floor lacrosse.

Photo 3.9 An adaptation of table cricket played at floor level

DISABILITY (continued)

- A tennis ball could be taped under the heel of a non-disabled young person to simulate an impairment. Parachute games are also useful.
- Young people can hold the parachute up and move underneath it by swapping places.
- A group can create a billowed tent effect and sit underneath it (and swap places).
- A young person can sit on top of the parachute and be wrapped in it.
- The group can release the parachute so it lands and folds onto a young person.
- You can create your own using a flat bed sheet and cut holes in the sheet to aid a different dimension to the game.
- If a home-made parachute with holes is used, certain balls can only go down particular holes, or you have to defend the hole, or it is competitive between four people trying to score in their half of the sheet. As the sheet is smaller, the activity becomes more skilful for those who are using it.

Photo 3.10 A flat sheet could be utilised for parachute games with small groups

Games for young people who may have difficulty with upper body movement and control

Key considerations

This list is in no particular order, nor is it essential to complete each and every time. It provides suggestions of some of the ways in which you can support the young person in your class. Some may be more relevant than others, so select what may work best for you. Safety and safe practice are paramount throughout, and only you know what is appropriate for the young people in your PE lessons.

Before the lesson

- Where possible give an indication of what you will be doing before the actual lesson. This can be given in advance, potentially 24 hours before, especially if the young person is anxious.
- Ask the young person to contribute to your ideas of inclusion. Empower them.
- Ask the young person if they wish to work with a friend/group for particular activities. Consider doing this discreetly at first if you do not know the young person.
- Ask the young person if they wish for you to share some do's and don'ts to the class about limb movement. The young person may wish to lead this but allow them the choice. Create an atmosphere where peers feel comfortable to ask questions to increase awareness of the young person's particular learning needs in a positive, considerate way.
- Consider the sports/activities on the curriculum: are there better, more inclusive activities that could be trialled or included?
- Encourage peers to work in consideration of the young person who may have additional needs especially if they can see the young person may be in danger. Specific instructions could be given to one peer to help clarify information given by the teacher to the young person.
- It is valuable to allow all young people to experience working with others outside of their friendship group.

During the lesson

- Be mindful of balance.
- Check in with the young person on their engagement/preference.
- Other body parts may be used instead (if appropriate).

(Continued)

- Encourage the young person to ask for clarity if necessary.

- Allow rest breaks if the young person seems anxious.

- Make sure the young person is being challenged in the activity you have set.

After the lesson

- Allow the young person to provide feedback on what worked well for them.

- Seek out if the young person felt challenged enough, did their skills improve?

- Personally reflect on the suitability of your lesson.

OPEN – everyone can be included with very little modification

- If the young person is unable to receive or pass objects, allow peer/teaching assistant to assist in this and their balance. Ask the young person first what they feel most comfortable with. Allow the young person to provide options that they will feel comfortable with in adapting the activity, for example, using feet, different objects, and use of support aid.
- If warm-ups require throwing, encourage the young person to explore how they can send items and receive them with different body parts. Allow larger, softer equipment to propel in the first instance.
- See resource card C.

MODIFIED – Using changes to Space, Task, Equipment, People (STEP) to include all

- Distance of items to be propelled needs to be considered.
- In net games, consider the size of the court and differentiate between abilities providing more or less space as appropriate.
- Provide a channel or space where the young person may be uncontested to gain confidence.
- Some young people will enjoy contact sport and others may not. If a young person does not want contact, then consider ways to tag the player; for example, use a bib or rugby tag belt.
- Allow a pair to play as one against an opposition.
- If the young person wishes to score goals, place a target that is attached to the post/net/goal so they have a differentiated version of a goal.
- Allow a variety of different sized or weighted balls to allow easier control and easier balance of the young person.
- Using striking tees will make striking the ball easier.
- Use balloons or balloon balls to mimic badminton, so play with body parts propelling the balloon ball over the net. Progress to other lighter balls to provide further challenge.
- Implement small-sided activities to reduce pressure.
- Allow a double bounce if necessary.

■ A variety of different skills could be isolated for all young people in order to refine a skill.

Example 1

Activity 1

■ A station where the young person can explore striking a ball with different body parts.

Activity 2

■ A station where the young person can explore striking a variety of different sized and weighted balls from high and low positions.

Activity 3

■ Allow each young person to use their preferred way of sending an object in a practice aiming at a target or 'going for distance'.

Activity 4

■ Devise a way of scoring so that each team member can contribute.

Activity 5

■ Different sized balls have to be kicked from a rounder's batting position. Once all six balls have been kicked, run around as many times in the time it takes fielders to collect the balls and return to a nominated person or place. Change the distance of running area if balance is an issue.

Example 2

Activity 1

■ Allow the young person to find ways to trap a balloon ball with their body. Try to develop this into a ball of their choice.

Activity 2

■ Find a way to send the ball trap/receive it without using hands.

Activity 3

■ Allow the young person to play an adapted game alongside netball, rugby, etc. that has similar principles to the selected game, so that all can play and contribute in their own way.

SPECIFIC – purposeful related activity to develop or enhance a skill

■ Develop passing with feet or different body parts to increase confidence.
■ Send to a solid feature, for example, a wall until more comfortable with the skill.
■ Line up a number of balls that the young people can kick in the direction of the wall. Working with a teaching assistant the young person can gather all balls back up together or alone.
■ To develop passing accuracy, use cones/spot mats/chalk and gradually decrease the angle of the scoring channel; for example, the balls on the edge should encourage the young person to slightly alter their body position to make sure balls stay within the scoring channel.

DISABILITY – introducing disability-specific sports

Reverse integration
■ Encourage young people to consider how they can modify a game so scoring can be achieved without using their upper body.

Additional resources
■ Promote http://limbpower.com/.

4 Gymnastics

Karen Broughton and Lerverne Barber

Gymnastics offers young people the opportunity to be creative as they explore movements individually, with a partner and in groups, with or without the use of apparatus. They are also encouraged to evaluate performances: their own and others'. Therefore, when considering adaptations, you will need to reflect on any changes that may be required in relation to any compositional and evaluation tasks (where appropriate) as well as performance skills. The section below focusses mainly on suggestions regarding adaptations for performance-related skills and tasks; however, there are some additional ideas for use when undertaking compositional and evaluation work.

Obviously safety is paramount when teaching Physical Education, and gymnastics has additional safety implications, owing to the nature of the content and use of specific apparatus. Any gymnastic activity and identified adaptations need to be carefully considered *before* the lesson. Wherever possible, these should be discussed with the young person so that appropriate progressions can be planned for, and any additional resources to support and enhance learning can be identified.

This section of the handbook focusses on the four key movement areas as points to consider when teaching gymnastics:

- **Travelling** – using different body parts, directions, speed, body shape, etc.

- **Rotation** – rolling and turning around different body parts, axis and equipment, etc.

- **Balance** – using different body parts, different body shapes, with others, on apparatus, etc.

- **Flight** – jumping, take-off and landings, body shape, etc.

All of the above consider:

- The use of apparatus – on/off/over/through apparatus

- The use of handheld gymnastic apparatus such as ribbons and hoops, etc.

- Working individually, with partners and groups

- The use of compositional tasks to link movements together to create gymnastic sequences

■ Evaluation tasks to help improve the quality of the work

All of the usual safe practice considerations for gymnastics such as warming up, safe handling and use of apparatus and safe and appropriate skill progressions must be planned for and adhered to throughout.

Photo 4.1 Stretching as part of the warm-up at the start of the lesson

Gymnastics for young people who may have difficulty seeing, even when wearing glasses

Key considerations

This list is in no particular order, nor is it essential to complete each and every time. It provides suggestions for **some** of the ways in which you can support the young person in your class. Some may be more relevant than others, so select what may work best for you. Safety and safe practice are paramount throughout, and only you know what is appropriate for the young people in your PE lessons.

Before the lesson

■ Where possible, give an indication of what you will be doing before the actual lesson. This can be given in advance, potentially 24 hours, especially if the young person is anxious.

■ Ask the young person to contribute to your ideas of inclusion. Empower them.

(Continued)

■ Ask the young person if they wish to work with a friend/group for particular activities. Consider doing this discreetly at first if you do not know the young person.

■ Ask the young person if they wish for you to share some do's and don'ts to the class about visual awareness. The young person may wish to lead this but allow them the choice. Create an atmosphere where the class feel comfortable to ask questions about visual awareness in a positive, considerate way.

■ Trust between the teacher, the young person and their peers is important, as the young person may be nervous about moving or jumping in the space.

■ Encourage peers to work in consideration of the young person who may have additional needs particularly if they can see the young person may be in danger. Specific instructions could be given to one peer to help clarify information given by the teacher to the young person.

■ It is valuable to allow all young people to experience working with others outside of their friendship group.

During the lesson

■ Allow the young person to orientate themselves in an area and ask others to be mindful and respectful of this.

■ To define a safe area for the young person to work in, use flat throw down markers on the floor, or tape with string beneath it to allow the young person to guide with their foot/hand.

■ Gymnastics can be a strongly visual activity; however, it can be experienced through touch. Being able to feel an apparatus will help the young person to orientate themselves.

■ It may be better if the young person stands closer to the teacher initially when giving instructions.

■ If they want to, and the teacher agrees, allow them to place their hands on the teacher in order to understand the movements better.

■ To introduce an idea or explain a skill, pictures can be used with the addition of Braille text and videos will need to include commentary. If the young person has some sight with the use of adaptations, for example, can see particular colours, this can be included when using images, such as for resource cards.

Photo 4.2 A range of surfaces offer young people a chance to explore different textures; this might need to be done with support initially

When **performing movements** and **sequences**:

■ Provide clear teaching points and additional descriptions to explain how to perform particular actions.

■ Enable the young person to use touch in order to get a better sense of the shape of a movement or what it means to extend limbs fully for example.

■ See below for considerations and/or adaptations to specific types of movement.

When **creating sequences**:

■ Provide additional feedback – teacher or a peer – in order to ensure that the movements selected are appropriate for the gymnastic theme.

■ Allow more time when creating sequences for other performers, and have a peer to talk through the movements/sequence as they are performed, to ensure that it is an accurate reflection of the young person's intentions.

■ Use clear teaching points to highlight the use of specific movements and/or the focus of the composition.

■ Allow more time to process and orientate.

■ Learning outcomes should be broad enough to allow all pupils the opportunity to be challenged but to successfully achieve them.

(Continued)

When **evaluating gymnastic performances**:

■ Use commentary to describe what, how and where in the space the movements are being performed.

■ Ask peers to narrate what they see in a performance.

■ It may be helpful to 'freeze-frame' the sequence at various points and support the young person to move around the space, using touch to identify body positions and the use of the space. This will help the young person to build up a set of images in their mind of different points within the sequence, in order to have a clearer overall understanding of the performance.

■ Perform the sequence in silence so that the young person can listen to the sounds made on the floor and give feedback regarding control on landings.

■ Allow the young person to describe their own moves if they do not wish to perform.

After the lesson

■ Allow the young person to provide feedback on what worked well for them.

■ Seek out if the young person felt challenged enough, did their cognition improve?

■ Personally reflect on the suitability of your lesson.

All of the suggestions below will be in the context of exploring movements in relation to a specific gymnastic theme, and performing, creating and evaluating gymnastic sequences as outlined so far.

Photo 4.3 Balancing on small body parts could be a good challenge to set some young people and they will answer it in their own way

---

OPEN – everyone can be included with very little modification

Travelling

- Can use a tether if the young person does not wish to hold hands, or use shoulder or elbow if preferred.
- Section off an area and explain to all that this is a safe movement channel/area for the young person.
- If there is some sight, place bright colours on the wall to aid directional sense.

Rotation

- Section off an area and explain to all young people this is a safe movement channel/area for the young person.
- Guide the young person through the movement first with your words.
- Explain the requirements of rolling/turning and direction of travel. What body part moves first, what is the starting position, etc. Support throughout the move as appropriate. This can be mapped out onto their hands if necessary.

Balance

- Ask the young person if they require a guide for support as balance may be affected.
- Use a wall, movement table, etc. if necessary. The young person may prefer to sit down.
- Allow the young person to explore a range of balances in their own time, and guide the movement exploration with suggestions.

Flight

- Allow the young person to explore a range of jumps and leaps using self-discovery teaching style.
- Offer support initially to increase confidence in terms of safe landings.
- If travel is required into the jump, explain distance before commencing the jump.

MODIFIED – Using changes to Space, Task, Equipment, People (STEP) to include all

Travelling

- Use of throw down markers/ropes to encourage the development of pathways when travelling or to provide specific areas to work in.
- Slowly increase/vary the pace of the travelling action.
- Does the young person have to be on their feet to travel? They may feel more secure when they are stationary with other young people moving around them. The young person may wish to travel in a different way. Can this be incorporated into the lesson?
- Throw down markers will be useful to assist with positioning.
- Consider adding more or less young people together to create a sequence.

Rotation

- Allow the young person to orientate themselves in the space first.
- Encourage the young person to point in the direction they intend to turn.
- Introduce simple rolling actions first, for example, log rolls and tucked rolls.
- Increase rotation gradually and only if appropriate e.g. 180°–360°.
- Use support to increase stability and confidence.

MODIFIED (continued)

Balance

- Review earlier suggestions.
- Does the young person need to be off the floor to balance? Can they use a line or wide bench (if levels are being taught?)

Flight

- Review earlier suggestions.
- Start with jumping on the spot to begin with, holding a partner/teacher's hand for additional support and to ensure a safe landing.
- If, using a springboard, the measurement of distance to the equipment can be walked and rehearsed, and only when trust and confidence is established, should a supported jump be attempted.

PARALLEL – activities delivered simultaneously which allow for different starting points

Travelling

Travelling movements can be attempted in different stages (low, medium and high) so all young people can decide which mode of travel they prefer. The young person could then pair up and try to mirror or contrast the moves so as to learn to support each other. Tethers can be used to help guide the 'levels' being explored.

- Examples of low levels: crawling, crab walk, sliding on stomach, sideways log/pencil roll, tucked/ barrel roll, etc.
- Examples of medium levels: bear walk, caterpillar walk, forward and backward rolls, sideways shoulder roll, etc.
- Examples of high levels: galloping, hopping, jumping, etc.

Rotation

- Introduce the concept of rolling via the use of a toy such as a teddy bear or a doll, which can be manipulated to roll forwards, enabling the young person to 'feel' the action of roll. Encourage the young person to explore basic rolls first, for example, log or pencil, tucked or barrel, before building confidence and moving to the more difficult rolls, such as straddle roll, sideways shoulder roll, forward roll, etc.

Photo 4.4 Using a hoop enables young people to think more broadly when exploring rotation in gymnastic sequences

PARALLEL (continued)

- Task cards are a useful resource and should be read out to the young person or provided in large font/Braille (if appropriate).
- If the young person is uncomfortable about rolling, consider other forms of rotation with different body parts and/or using small apparatus such as a hoop.

Balance

- Introduce the concept of levels (e.g. low, medium and high) within balancing, and encourage the young person to explore balance using the low levels on a variety of body parts, starting with, 'patches' (large body parts, stomach, back, bottom, shoulders, etc.) before building confidence and moving to 'points', that is, small body parts (hands, feet, knees, elbows, etc.) Levels can be introduced this way, and the young person can then explore and discover a range of body shapes in their balances and the use of apparatus, for example, leaning against a box for support or balancing over/along a bench.

Flight

- The young person can explore flight off the ground, onto, off and over small and large equipment, for example, springboards, vaults, a range of gym tables, etc. according to their ability.
- Encourage the young person to vary their shape in flight, even if from a low height. Shape can be modified by arms alone.

SPECIFIC – purposeful related activity to develop or enhance a skill

Travelling

- With a partner or teaching assistant, use a section of the gym space that they have sole use of, in order to develop confidence of travelling using different pathways, different levels and, if possible, different speeds. Only use this if the young person needs to continue to build their confidence.

Rotation

- Obtain individual support and guidance from the teacher or a teaching assistant to develop confidence of rolling. If a teaching assistant is supporting, they will need to be overseen to ensure health and safety is not compromised. Consider the most appropriate rolls necessary to instil confidence, challenge and success (see earlier suggestions for progression through the different rolls, beginning with sideways).

Balance

- Working with a partner/teaching assistant or apparatus to develop confidence in balancing, allow practise time. There are teaching assistant cards available for this (13, 14).

Flight

- Suggest that unless low-level flight is the objective, this activity and progressions should only be supervised by the class teacher, and therefore, this is more challenging to do as a separate activity for the young person. Earlier adaptions may be more appropriate.

Reverse integration

■ Allow others in the group to have partial sight loss by wearing either adapted sunglasses or blindfolds, and perform simple tasks in pairs, such as slowly travelling in the space.

■ Encourage the sighted young people to constantly describe what they are doing.

Additional resources

■ Promote the website https://britishblindsport.org.uk/ for elite pathways as well as advice on making mainstream clubs more aware of support for young people that have difficulty seeing, even when wearing glasses.

Gymnastics for young people who may have hearing difficulty, even when using a hearing aid. This can also incorporate linguistic difficulties

Key considerations

This list is in no particular order, nor is it essential to complete each and every time. It provides suggestions of *some* of the ways in which you can support the young person in your class. Some may be more relevant than others, so select what may work best for you. Safety and safe practice are paramount throughout, and only you know what is appropriate for the young people in your PE lessons.

Before the lesson

■ Where possible, give an indication of what you will be doing before the actual lesson. This can be given in advance, potentially 24 hours, especially if the young person is anxious.

■ Ask the young person to contribute to your ideas of inclusion. Empower them.

■ Ask the young person if they wish to work with a friend/group for particular activities. Consider doing this discreetly at first if you do not know the young person.

■ Ask the young person if they wish for you to share some do's and don'ts to the class about D/deaf awareness. The young person may wish to lead this but allow them the choice. Create an atmosphere where the class feel comfortable to ask questions about D/deaf awareness in a positive, considerate way.

■ Consider teaching some basic signs that the whole class can use.

■ Not every Deaf person knows sign language, not every Deaf person can read lips and not every Deaf person is oral.

■ Encourage peers to work in consideration of the young person who may have additional needs especially if they can see the young person may be in danger. Specific instructions could be given to one peer to help clarify information given by the teacher to the young person.

■ It is valuable to allow all young people to experience working with others outside of their friendship group.

In addition to the above, there may be specific consideration for young people with linguistic disabilities:

■ The use of Picture Exchange Communication System (PECS) could be valuable, for example, where possible, consider having photos or pictures of what you intend to use or what you want the young person to do and achieve within the lesson. This could be presented in a list so the young person can tick off the items as they go. Microsoft Immersive Reader provides images and translations that may help.

■ Consider giving the young person a copy of the photos/pictures too; this may include emotions so that the young person can flick to the emotions that they wish to express.

During the lesson

■ When giving instructions, speak in a clear and regular tone of voice ensuring that the young person can see your face and lips.

■ There is no need to exaggerate your volume or speak too slowly.

■ Demonstrate *everything*!

■ Try to use more visual gestures, body language and facial expressions rather than relying on words to communicate.

■ Use visual cues for different points in the lesson that all pupils become familiar with and respond to, for example, for starting and stopping points in the lesson.

■ Keep instructions literal and try to avoid abstract concepts.

■ Monitor that the young person is not isolated. Consider what you will do if you spot this and how you will address it.

When **performing** and **creating** gymnastic skills and sequences:

■ Provide lots of demonstrations, teacher, peers and video examples.

■ Use resource cards to support the instructions provided with images and text (if the young person can read).

When **evaluating** gymnastic performances:

■ Use task cards to describe what to look for when observing other's work and/or evaluating own performances.

(Continued)

There are additional considerations **if using music to create and perform** the gymnastic sequences:

■ Depending on the level of hearing the young person has, they may be able to hear sounds/music; however, each young person will hear different things, not necessarily always the strongest bass or loudest sounds. They may sense the bass, certain pitches or particular instruments.

■ The young person may be able to feel vibrations through different objects within the room or by touching the speakers.

■ Young people may have found different ways to feel music through sensation from different body parts and environmental factors. Therefore, consideration of the type of music/accompaniment is important.

■ If you are using music, ask the young person to conduct a sound check before the lesson starts; they may want to alter where they stand in the space depending on the type of music being used.

■ Think about ways to clap or gesture the tempo of the music to help the young person internalise the speed and tempo.

■ It may also be helpful to tap on the young person's arm or shoulder to demonstrate the rhythm or the beat of the music.

After the lesson

■ Allow the young person to communicate back to you or peers in a variety of ways; they can draw, write, demonstrate or use translate options on various apps.

■ Seek out if the young person felt challenged enough, did their skills improve?

■ Personally reflect on the suitability of your lesson.

OPEN – everyone can be included with very little modification

Travelling, rotation, balance and flight

■ Provide a brief lesson plan beforehand so that the young person can refer to it throughout the lesson.

■ Allow the pupil to follow a peer if it is an exploration warm-up.

■ Use clear visual demonstrations or use images displayed on a mobile device, so that the young person can access to review the movement if necessary.

■ Ensure the class/group is aware of how to attract the attention of the young person.

■ Use open-ended questions to check understanding.

Photo 4.5 Allow young people to explore their surroundings including using different apparatus as appropriate

MODIFIED – Using changes to Space, Task, Equipment, People (STEP) to include all

Travelling, rotation, balance and flight

■ It should not be necessary for any further modifications, unless the young person has other specific needs (see other sections). All of the suggestions in the previous sections should enable the young person to successfully take part in the same activity as their peers.

DISABILITY – introducing disability-specific sports

Reverse integration

■ Teacher to teach the lesson using no voice at all.
■ Allow pupils to talk to each other if need be (or not at all!), but they cannot ask the teacher anything unless they do not use their voice; they have to use gestures or demonstrations, or write things down.

Additional resources

■ Visit and promote https://ukdeafsport.org.uk/.
■ Young people who have hearing difficulty can join mainstream clubs if coaches are deaf aware. British gymnastics does support Deaf Sport (https://ukdeafsport.org.uk/british-gymnastics-support-deafinitely-inclusive/)

*** It is not necessary to consider PARALLEL or SPECIFIC activities in relation to this task/activity.*

Gymnastics for young people who may have difficulty remembering or concentrating

Key considerations

This list is in no particular order, nor is it essential to complete each and every time. It provides suggestions of **some** of the ways in which you can support the young person in your class. Some may be more relevant than others, so select what may work best for you. Safety and safe practice are paramount throughout, and only you know what is appropriate for the young people in your PE lessons.

Before the lesson

- Where possible, give an indication of what you will be doing before the actual lesson. This can be given in advance, potentially 24 hours, especially if the young person is anxious.

- Ask the young person to contribute to your ideas of inclusion. Empower them.

- Ask the young person if they wish to work with a friend/group for particular activities. Consider doing this discreetly at first if you do not know the young person.

- Ask the young person if they wish for you to share some do's and don'ts to the class about their specific needs. The young person may wish to lead this but allow them the choice. Create an atmosphere where the class feel comfortable to ask questions about the young person's specific learning needs in a positive, considerate way.

- Consider having PECS to assist with equipment and order of activities ahead of and throughout the session if appropriate. Microsoft Immersive Reader can also help put words into pictures, as well as translate.

- Encourage peers to work in consideration of the young person who may have additional needs especially if they can see the young person may be in danger. Specific instructions could be given to one peer to help clarify information given by the teacher to the young person.

- It is valuable to allow all young people to experience working with others outside of their friendship group.

- If music is being used, for example, in the warm-up or for the creation of sequence work, ask the young person to listen to it in advance of the lesson, perhaps give it to them to play at home so that they become familiar with what to expect. This will help to reduce any anxiety.

During the lesson

■ The main focus of the lesson may need to be revisited a number of times to remind the young person.

■ It might be useful to provide the young person with resources with the task written and/or drawn for the young person to refer to.

■ If music is too much of a distraction for the young person, try using it intermittently rather than continuously and/or adjusting the volume.

■ When giving instructions, speak clearly and try not to give too much information at once.

■ Develop well-established routines with cues for different aspects of the lesson, for example, different coloured scarfs to wave or a specific sound such as a percussion instrument to stop and start an activity.

■ Try to keep the pace of the lesson brisk, but remember to allow additional time for the young person to process the information if appropriate.

■ Ensure that the challenges created for the young person are achievable, but not too easy.

■ Provide lots of praise and constructive feedback to build self-esteem and self-confidence.

■ Teaching assistants can support the young person to understand and remember the task and maintain focus.

■ Provide a list of activities that will be experienced and ask the young person to tick them off as they proceed through the lesson.

■ Provide a glossary of terms to aid understanding.

■ Encourage the young person to ask for clarity if necessary.

■ Reference TV characters (as suggested in Appendix A) that may support the young person in visualising and copying particular actions.

■ Allow rest breaks if the young person seems anxious.

When **performing** and **creating** gymnastic sequences:

■ Provide lots of demonstrations, teacher, peers or video examples in order to improve understanding and aid memory.

■ Use resource cards to support the instructions provided with images and text (if the young person can read).

■ Allow additional time to practise and repeat movements and to remember compositions.

(Continued)

Photo 4.6 Through progressive activities, appropriate support and practise, young people will increase their movement vocabulary and acquire a wider range of skills

When **evaluating** gymnastic skills and sequences:

- Use very specific criteria of what to look for in the performance when observing other's work and/or evaluating own performances. This may need to be reinforced in different ways, for example, through demonstration and via individual resource cards.

- Allow time for the young person to reflect on what they have seen and organise their thoughts. Use keywords on a whiteboard or a resource sheet to help them formulate appropriate feedback to the performers being evaluated or in response to a pre-recorded gymnastic performance.

- If appropriate, work with a peer to support the evaluation and feedback process.

After the lesson

- Allow the young person to provide feedback on what worked well for them.

- Seek out if the young person felt challenged enough, did their understanding/cognition improve?

- Personally reflect on the suitability of your lesson.

OPEN – everyone can be included with very little modification

Travelling, rotation, balance and flight

■ Use diagrams/photos/films and demonstrations if necessary to support understanding further.
■ Allow someone else in the class to go first, so the young person can copy the actions/requirements.
■ Create a safe channel should the young person need it and explain this area to peers.
■ Send an outline of the lesson to the teaching assistant and/or young person 24 hours prior to the lesson.

MODIFIED – Using changes to Space, Task, Equipment, People (STEP) to include all

Travelling, rotation, balance and flight

■ Be flexible with the amount of space available for the young person to explore how their body may move in each of the actions (they may need to have an increased amount of personal space).
■ Seek clarity to see if the young person may wish more or less space.
■ Balance and confidence may be compromised, so modify activity to empower and/or offer additional support and/or more practise time in the early stages. As the young person develops their confidence, more challenges can be set.
■ Allow the young person to continue to explore how they can modify or interpret the task for themselves.
■ Explanations may take longer to be processed, so allow more time for each task/activity (if required).
■ Slowly increase/vary the pace of the travelling actions.
■ Use PECS to help aid memory of sequences.
■ Suggest a range of equipment to provide options that the young person can build from.
■ If the same lesson outcomes can be achieved from a standing/seated/lower/supported position, then allow the use of equipment to modify the activity.

PARALLEL – activities delivered simultaneously which allow for different starting points

Travelling, rotation, balance and flight

■ See suggestions mentioned in previous parallel sections earlier in this chapter.
■ Phase in suggestions, adaptations and travelling ideas to avoid overloading the young person.
■ Allow practise time and a friend to help repeat aspects should the young person need.
■ Use pictures, for example using PECS to help construct a gymnastic sequence before practising it. This should help the young person in terms of understanding and being able to memorise the sequence.

(Continued)

Travelling, rotation, balance and flight

■ Use instruction sheets for teaching assistants so that they can engage the young person if they go off-task or misinterpret the activity.
■ Allow peers to work with the young person where possible so that they are not always segregated from the entire class. This works particularly well when exploring movement (this can be done in pairs) and when developing paired or small group sequences.

Photo 4.7 Working with peers can encourage creativity and develop positive relationships

Reverse integration

■ Create an activity where you overload your class with information such as a noise stimulus, inaccurate information and time pressure. This may allow their peers to be aware of anxiety issues when processing information.

Additional resources

■ You can raise awareness of a number of organisations, and this could be an opportunity for you to promote mainstream sport, as well as impairment-specific competitive pathways such as the Special Olympics. Try:
■ https://www.mencap.org.uk/about-us/what-we-do/mencap-sport
■ http://www.uksportsassociation.org/
■ https://www.specialolympics.org/
■ https://www.british-gymnastics.org/discover/disability-gymnastics

Gymnastics for young people who may have difficulty walking or climbing stairs

Key considerations

This list is in no particular order, nor is it essential to complete each and every time. It provides suggestions of **some** of the ways in which you can support the young person in your class. Some may be more relevant than others, so select what may work best for you. Safety and safe practice are paramount throughout, and only you know what is appropriate for the young people in your PE lessons.

Before the lesson

- Where possible give an indication of what you will be doing before the actual lesson. This can be given in advance, potentially 24 hours, especially if the young person is anxious.
- Ask the young person to contribute to your ideas of inclusion. Empower them.
- Ask the young person if they wish to work with a friend/group for particular activities. Consider doing this discreetly at first if you do not know the young person.
- Ask the young person if they wish for you to share some do's and don'ts to the class about wheelchair etiquette. The young person may wish to lead this but allow them the choice. Create an atmosphere where the class feel comfortable to ask questions about awareness of the young person's particular learning needs in a positive, considerate way.
- Encourage peers to work in consideration of the young person who may have additional needs especially if they can see the young person may be in danger. Specific instructions could be given to one peer to help clarify information given by the teacher to the young person.
- It is valuable to allow all young people to experience working with others outside of their friendship group.

During the lesson

- When creating gymnastic group sequences, the young person may need additional resources in order to effectively communicate their ideas for movements that they may find difficult to demonstrate themselves. You can support this by enabling young people to have access to YouTube during the lesson, in order that they can find examples of movements they would like to include in their compositions, but that they may not be able to clearly explain either verbally or through their own demonstrations.

(Continued)

■ Build up a bank of online resources for all young people to access.

■ Create a glossary of terms, and use appropriate terminology frequently when discussing work or creating evaluation resources for pupils to use. This will support all pupils to develop their understanding of gymnastic movement vocabulary and compositional principles when creating gymnastic sequences. This will also support pupils' ability to evaluate gymnastic performances.

■ Remember that if the learning outcomes are broad enough, the young person should be able to answer the task with minimal adaption. For example, if the outcome is *to explore different types of jumps*, this may be very difficult for some young people to achieve. However, if the learning outcome is *to explore different ways of travelling in the space*, then pupils, including those who have restricted mobility, can be encouraged to use a range of different movements to meet this outcome. This does not mean that they won't still be challenged to explore a wider range of movements and also continue to improve the quality of their performance.

■ Allow rest breaks of necessary.

After the lesson

■ Allow the young person to provide feedback on what worked well for them.

■ Seek out if the young person felt challenged enough.

■ Personally reflect on the suitability of your lesson.

OPEN – everyone can be included with very little modification

Travelling

■ If, using a wheelchair, allow the young person to self-propel around the area (if possible). Consider left- and right-hand pushing, and reversing, one push turns to create a 360° as a way of travel. Can still travel under larger items and over ramps (gym mat if secured).
■ Create a pattern on the floor for the young person to steer/navigate around with various floor patterns to create challenge. Investigate different speeds.
■ Discuss how comfortable the young person feels about moving around the area in a variety of different ways. This could involve using assistive walking devices or allow movement along the floor or on top of things of a low level.
■ Break down the movement and allow repetition of actions before moving on.
■ Try to include movements that use opposite hand to opposite leg and cross the child's midline, for example, crawling if appropriate.
■ Encourage the young person to develop their travelling actions using both left- and right-sided dominant actions, for example, galloping action leading with the right foot and then the left foot.

OPEN (continued)

Rotation

■ Section off an area so that the young person can move freely in and out of their chair for rolling actions (if the young person is comfortable with this).

■ Encourage variations in speed and pathways when performing turning actions in chair or on foot with assistance.

■ As above, communicate with the young person regarding the pace/control of chair/how the young person moves.

■ Discuss with the young person what their range of movements is; how they would like to roll, turn and spin and what body parts might they use.

■ Break down the movements and allow repetition of actions before moving on.

Balance

■ Allow the young person to balance on aspects of the gym equipment to provide additional support.

■ Discuss with the young person what their range of movements is and how they would like to balance, for example, what body parts.

■ Break down the movements and allow repetition of action before moving on.

■ Ask the young person if they will allow peers to touch their chair/walker and potentially use it to balance against and/or utilise it as a base during sequence work.

Flight

■ Discuss with the young person what their range of movements is and whether they are able to jump, and if so, what types of jumps and what body shapes they might be able to make.

■ Discuss whether they would feel comfortable using equipment such as springboards and how support could be used to build confidence.

■ If the young person wishes to remain in a supported position (chair/walker), consider how they can move other parts of their body in relation to arm/head shapes created through flight.

MODIFIED – Using changes to Space, Task, Equipment, People (STEP) to include all

Travelling, rotation, balance and flight

■ See previous suggestions for modified activities and also open activities above.

■ Although the young person may have a more limited range of travel, it will be the quality of control, pose and creativity where the young person can be challenged further.

■ Gym equipment needs to be set out so the young person can go over, round and under things using a walker or chair.

■ Discuss and consider a set station for the young person to familiarise themselves with different ways to pull, drag and roll.

■ Use of throw down hands and feet markers or a line to map out the movement on the floor, and allow the young person to track and follow the markers.

■ Use of gymnastic equipment to develop and support the movement, for example, soft play shape tunnel to support pencil rolls, Swiss ball to develop the forward rocking motion (in preparation for the forward roll), etc.

PARALLEL – activities delivered simultaneously which allow for different starting points

Travelling, rotation, balance and flight

■ See previous suggestions for parallel activities and also modified/open in this section.

SPECIFIC – purposeful related activity to develop or enhance a skill

■ If the teacher feels that it is too difficult to modify activities, then consider a separate, purposeful activity, but discuss this with the young person, as they may not want to be segregated from their friends, but might be happy to work alongside with another similar task. Ask yourself if any of the outcomes of the lesson can be transferable into a more purposeful activity. For example, a young person with significant movement limitations may not want, nor be physically able, to experience the aspect of flight. Therefore, a different aspect/learning outcome, in a group or separate, would be far more relevant and purposeful, such as an activity that developed strength over small to larger barriers in a gym setting.

■ Some young people in wheelchairs are turning to more extreme sports, if the young person is keen to try flight and the relevant safeguarding has taken place, then consider supporting the young person into moving/flying safely, for example, parkour for young people in wheelchairs. Check out Aaron Fotheringham at https://www.youtube.com/watch?v=UQuBzShOFew.

■ There is a teaching assistant card that may help with this activity for balancing (14).

DISABILITY – introducing disability-specific sports

Reverse integration

■ Allow other students in the class to only move on one leg or use one arm to provide an example of difference. Allow them to explore what they think they can do.

Additional resources

■ Raise awareness of national governing bodies (WheelPower, Cerebral Palsy, Dwarf Sports, etc.) and consider local or regional development groups:
  o https://www.wheelpower.org.uk/ includes powerchair activities
  o http://www.cpsport.org/ includes framed activities
  o https://www.dsauk.org/
  o http://limbpower.com/
■ Also look at mainstream national governing bodies as some do have disability strands.
■ Developmental coordination disorder (dyspraxia) has an informative website:
  o http://elearning.canchild.ca/dcd_workshop/sports.html
■ https://www.british-gymnastics.org/discover/disability-gymnastics
■ Parkour for young people in wheelchairs: https://www.youtube.com/watch?v=UQuBzShOFew

Gymnastics for young people who may have difficulty with upper body movement or control

Key considerations

This list is in no particular order, nor is it essential to complete each and every time. It provides suggestions of *some* of the ways in which you can support the young person in your class. Some may be more relevant than others, so select what may work best for you. Safety and safe practice are paramount throughout, and only you know what is appropriate for the young people in your PE lessons.

Before the lesson

■ Where possible, give an indication of what you will be doing before the actual lesson. This can be given in advance, potentially 24 hours, especially if the young person is anxious.

■ Ask the young person to contribute to your ideas of inclusion. Empower them.

■ Ask the young person if they wish to work with a friend/group for particular activities. Consider doing this discreetly at first if you do not know the young person.

■ Ask the young person if they wish for you to share some do's and don'ts to the class about limb movement. The young person may wish to lead this but allow them the choice. Create an atmosphere where the class feel comfortable to ask questions about the young person's particular learning needs in a positive, considerate way.

■ Consider the activities on the curriculum: are there better, more inclusive activities that could be trialled or included?

■ Encourage peers to work in consideration of the young person who may have additional needs especially if they can see the young person may be in danger. Specific instructions could be given to one peer to help clarify information given by the teacher to the young person.

■ It is valuable to allow all young people to experience working with others outside of their friendship group.

(Continued)

During the lesson

- Be mindful of balance.

- When creating gymnastic group sequence work, the young person may need additional resources in order to effectively communicate their ideas for movements that they may find difficult to demonstrate themselves. You can support this by enabling young people to have access to YouTube during the lesson, in order that they can find examples of movements they would like to include in their compositions, but that they may not be able to clearly explain either verbally or through their own demonstrations.

- Build up a bank of online resources for all pupils to access.

- Create a glossary of terms, and use appropriate terminology frequently when discussing work or creating evaluation resources for pupils to use. This will support all pupils to develop their understanding of gymnastic movement vocabulary and compositional principles when creating gymnastic sequences. This will also support pupil's ability to evaluate gymnastic performances.

- Remember that if the learning outcomes are broad enough, the young person should be able to answer the task with minimal adaptation. For example, if the outcome is *to explore different ways to take weight on hands*, this may be very difficult for some young people to achieve. However, if the learning outcome is *to explore different ways of supporting the body,* then all pupils, including those who have restricted mobility, can be encouraged to use a range of different movements to meet this outcome. This does not mean that they won't still be challenged to explore a wider range of movements and also continue to improve the quality of their performance, compositional skills and the ability to evaluate effectively.

- Check in with the young person on their engagement/preferences.

- Other body parts may be used instead (if appropriate).

- Encourage the young person to ask for clarity if necessary.

- Allow rest breaks if the young person seems anxious.

- Make sure the young person is being challenged in the activity you have set.

After the lesson

- Allow the young person to provide feedback on what worked well for them.

- Seek out if the young person felt challenged enough, did their skills improve?

- Personally reflect on the suitability of your lesson.

OPEN – everyone can be included with very little modification

Travelling

- The young person could attempt and be exposed to all travel movements (high, low, fast and slow).
- Discuss this with the young person beforehand.

Rotation

- Discuss with the young person what their range of movements is; how they would like to roll, turn and spin and what do they feel more/less comfortable about and why.

MODIFIED – Using changes to Space, Task, Equipment, People (STEP) to include all

Travelling, rotation, balance and flight

- It should not be necessary for any further modifications, unless the young person has other specific needs (see other sections). All of the suggestions in the previous sections should enable the young person to successfully take part in the same activity as their peers.

DISABILITY – introducing disability-specific sports

Additional resources

Refer to the website http://limbpower.com/.

*** It is not necessary to consider PARALLEL or SPECIFIC activities in relation to this task/activity.*

5 Outdoor and adventurous activities

Charlotte Beaman-Evans

Outdoor and Adventurous Activities is the term used in the Physical Education (PE) National Curriculum to describe common activities that can be taught on most school sites. In this handbook, we focus on school-based activities rather than the outdoor adventurous activities that would traditionally be delivered via a residential experience. We recognise that some schools have facilities that support a robust outdoor programme, and some teachers are qualified to offer this wider range of activities, but this is not the case for most schools in the UK. Therefore, the activities in this chapter have been selected to reflect the key areas commonly taught when schools have minimal equipment/facilities. We have focussed on orienteering via map reading, problem-solving and teamwork, and there are also examples of parachute games in Chapter 3 of this handbook, which teachers might want to refer to. All the activities can be used to improve pupil collaboration as well as in developing physical ability and communication skills, and encouraging all young people to work together to achieve a common goal.

The need to be able to trust others is an important starting point. The activities selected will be more successful if there is a positive working relationship between the young people in your class. Perhaps bonding sessions have already taken place to inform the selection of these suggested activities. Sensitivity should be considered as some young people with disabilities may find it hard to trust others, so scaffolding may be necessary, gradually progressing the ideas and skills as the young person becomes more confident.

Photo 5.1 Sharing good practice amongst colleagues is crucial

Each activity mentioned in this chapter has its own mini context. Key considerations for each identified disability are only outlined in the first activity −orienteering − as many of the suggestions apply to all the activities.

Activities include the following:

1. Orienteering −map reading and navigation skills

2. Problem-solving/communications skills − chasing the chicken rounders

3. Team building −giants, wizards, elves warm-up game

4. Cooperation and trust −rope of peace warm-up game

5. Teamwork −balloon balance

Activity 1: Problem-solving – map reading and navigation skills

Orienteering for young people who may have difficulty seeing, even when wearing glasses

Key considerations

This list is in no particular order, nor is it essential to complete each and every time. It provides suggestions of *some* of the ways in which you can support the young person in your class. Some may be more relevant than others, so select what may work best for you. Safety and safe practice are paramount throughout, and only you know what is appropriate for the young people in your PE lessons.

Before the lesson

■ Where possible, give an indication of what you will be doing before the actual lesson. This can be given in advance, potentially 24 hours, especially if the young person is anxious.

■ Ask the young person to contribute to your ideas of inclusion. Empower them.

■ Ask the young person if they wish to work with a friend/group for particular activities. Consider doing this discreetly at first if you do not know the young person.

■ Ask the young person if they wish for you to share some do's and don'ts to the class about visual awareness. The young person may wish to lead this but allow them the choice. Create an atmosphere where the class feel comfortable to ask questions about other's particular learning needs in a positive, considerate way.

(Continued)

- The use of brightly coloured equipment to assist with direction and highlighting obstacles is crucial. Planning of such equipment should be thought of ahead of the lesson to ensure these items are available.

- Allow the young person to have a safe word that can be used by all to protect each other, so the young person can orientate where people are around them. A common word is 'voy', meaning that I am close and know you are there but proceed with caution; the word is intended to be repeated over and over to give perspective of where the person is.

- Allow the young person to orientate themselves around the area.

- Laminate maps in case of bad weather. Paper copies will fray and tear in rain. Laminating will also avoid bends in the map, which, over a few hours, can become unreadable, leading to key features being overlooked.

- Be mindful of obstacles that may be part of the natural landscape that may be hazardous.

- Encourage peers to work in consideration of the young person who may have additional needs especially if they can see the young person may be in danger. Specific instructions could be given to one peer to help clarify information given by the teacher to the young person.

- It is valuable to allow all young people to experience working with others outside of their friendship group.

During the lesson

- If necessary, try to indicate the directions of movement by placing brightly coloured items for the young person to identify (brightly coloured pieces of card can be placed on walls/fences or secured on rounder's posts if outside).

- Encourage peers to 'look out' for the young person if they see them in danger.

- Check with the young person to see if they want to change partners.

- Observe if the young person is challenged enough. Observe if they appear to be isolated and decide how you may wish to address this.

- If there is a teaching assistant assigned to the young person, consider asking for an update of progress.

After the lesson

- Allow the young person to feedback on what worked well for them.

- Seek out if the young person felt challenged enough, did their skills improve?

- Personally reflect on the suitability of your lesson before planning the next one.

OPEN – everyone can be included with very little modification

■ Provide a Google Map that best portrays the area. Very often Google Maps better reflect the finer layout of buildings (e.g. school premises) and can be printed in a larger and clearer format than Ordinance Survey maps. Allow the young person to refer to it throughout the lesson.
■ Create, ahead of the lesson, a tactile map to depict changes of terrain so the young person can feel the range of distances they are asked to cover (if applicable).
■ Use 'read aloud' function on mobile devices to help with audio descriptions. 'Seeing AI' app for iPhones is one of many excellent tools.

MODIFIED – Using changes to Space, Task, Equipment, People (STEP) to include all

■ Identify the section of map being utilised. Enlarge and colour photocopy. All elements of the map including symbols, footpaths and key landmarks will be enlarged and more accessible for the young person.
■ Download an OS app (charge) to view a section of a map electronically and plot route.
■ Draw a map of a small area that can be navigated, for example, school playground/ adventure playground. Use old climbing rope to set up a rope course that is fixed to these features. Using the map the young person can plot their route through the course and then follow it. The rope being tied to the features will offer reassurance and something for the young person to hold onto and guide their way around the walk.
■ Create a large photograph of landmarks, so young people can look for landmarks that match the photo and travel there.
■ Key places are indicated brightly on the school site (fluorescent bib on a tree).
■ Ask the young person if they require a guide to help them navigate around the orienteering landscape (see Chapter 1 on track/running for advice).

PARALLEL – activities delivered simultaneously which allow for different starting points

■ Use photographs of the area that the young person will be navigating around. Trail photograph maps should reflect the route that the young person should follow.
■ Enlarge photos for viewing ease and add descriptions for a partner to read aloud. Encourage the young person to 'feel' aspects of the route as they go, for example, tree trunks, leaves coniferous and non-coniferous, fencing, walls, etc.
■ Opportunity for the young person to turn right or left should be identified with tactile symbols/photographs, for example, string taped to the laminated map indicating 'L' for left and 'R' for right turn.
■ Use a sighted peer or teaching assistant to read instructions/descriptions if appropriate or use 'read aloud' function on phones.

SPECIFIC – purposeful related activity to develop or enhance a skill

■ Use large and brightly coloured flash cards or tactile symbols using string taped to card of key map symbols. Encourage the young person to familiarise themselves with these symbols to the corresponding word. Could get the whole group to learn these.

= Footpath.

■ Create a tactile key and 3D map, and ask the young person to help design it. It could be a design and technology homework/classroom-based task for the whole class.

Reverse integration

■ This is an opportunity for the young person to teach the group Braille (if they themselves know it). Flashcards of symbols and corresponding words could be matched up with the new added challenge of matching up the Braille to the symbol/feature as well.
■ Lead each other around a course, building trust.

Photo 5.2 Sometimes taking young people out of their comfort zone is a valuable learning experience

Additional resources

■ See previous sections on links to Blind Sport but also view https://www.jasschools.org.uk/case-studies/987/
■ https://www.ramblers.org.uk/advice/walking-with-a-disability-or-health-issue/blind-and-partially-sighted-people.aspx

Orienteering for young people who may have hearing difficulty, even when using a hearing aid. This can also incorporate linguistic difficulties

Key considerations

This list is in no particular order, nor is it essential to complete each and every time. It provides suggestions of *some* of the ways in which you can support the young person in your class. Some may be more relevant than others, so select what may work best for you. Safety and safe practice are paramount throughout, and only you know what is appropriate for the young people in your PE lessons.

Before the lesson

- Where possible, give an indication of what you will be doing before the actual lesson. This can be given in advance, potentially 24 hours, especially if the young person is anxious.

- Ask the young person to contribute to your ideas of inclusion. Empower them.

- Ask the young person if they wish to work with a friend/group for particular activities. Consider doing this discreetly at first if you do not know the young person.

- Ask the young person if they wish for you to share some do's and don'ts to the class about D/deaf awareness. The young person may wish to lead this but allow them the choice. Create an atmosphere where the class feel comfortable to ask questions about D/deaf awareness in a positive, considerate way.

- Consider teaching some basic signs that the whole class can use.

- Not every deaf person knows sign language, not every Deaf person can read lips and not every Deaf person is oral.

- Encourage peers to work in consideration of the young person who may have additional needs especially if they can see the young person may be in danger. Specific instructions could be given to one peer to help clarify information given by the teacher to the young person.

- It is valuable to allow all young people to experience working with others outside of their friendship group.

- Laminate maps in case of bad weather. Paper copies will fray and tear in rain. Laminating will also avoid bends in the map, which, over a few hours, can become unreadable, leading to key features being overlooked.

(Continued)

Photo 5.3 Pre-planning before the lesson often aids inclusion

During the lesson

■ Use facial expression and hand/body gestures to assist with learning.

■ Demonstrate *everything*!

■ If using lines (follow the leader-type activities), allow the young person to be second in the queue so they can follow their peer, until they are comfortable.

■ Use visual commands (hand up to halt play instead of a whistle).

■ Ensure classmates are aware of changes/adaptations and ask them to cooperate when activity is stopped or to help reiterate instructions to the young person.

■ If working outside, consider any road crossings and inform the rest of the group to ensure they use traffic calming measures such as traffic lights or zebra crossings.

■ Be mindful of changes in terrain or areas that may cause more of a hazard underfoot.

■ Consider location and weather implications. Windy conditions and wet weather can affect hearing and may impact upon the young person's ability to lip-read.

■ Always consider where you stop and address the group and ensure the young person is in your sight and is able to see your face.

After the lesson

■ Allow the young person to feedback on what worked well for them.

■ Seek out if the young person felt challenged enough, did their cognition improve?

■ Personally reflect on the suitability of your lesson.

OPEN – everyone can be included with very little modification

■ Make sure the class are aware how to attract the attention of the young person who has a hearing impairment.
■ Make sure the pupils face the young person (if the young person reads lips).

MODIFIED – Using changes to Space, Task, Equipment, People (STEP) to include all

■ Encourage partner work if working on a school site or small group work to develop confidence in discussions and regarding map reading, including route plotting and pacing.
■ Identify 'legs' (section of route) that one person will lead and take responsibility for. This will allow for the young person to be in control without lots of background noise/chatter.
■ For longer distances, task small groups to design a visual trail (Appendix B) and allow others to do the same. Swap trails and follow (consider the terrain).

PARALLEL – activities delivered simultaneously which allow for different starting points

■ Use photographs of the area that the young person will be navigating around. Trail photograph maps should reflect the route that the young person should follow.
■ Each junction (opportunity for the young person to turn right or left) should be identified with annotated photographs.

SPECIFIC – purposeful related activity to develop or enhance a skill

■ As above.

DISABILITY – introducing disability-specific sports

Reverse integration

Opportunity for the young person to teach the group sign language (if sign language is known). Flashcards of symbols and corresponding words could be matched up with the new added challenge of demonstrating the corresponding sign language to match the symbol/feature.

Additional resources

Activities may be available on a more regional basis. Consider using the National Deaf Children's Society's website to assist in making connections:
https://www.ramblers.org.uk/advice/walking-with-a-disability-or-health-issue/deaf-and-hard-of-hearing-people.aspx

(Continued)

Orienteering for young people who may have difficulty remembering or concentrating

Key considerations

This list is in no particular order, nor is it essential to complete each and every time. It provides suggestions of **some** of the ways in which you can support the young person in your class. Some may be more relevant than others, so select what may work best for you. Safety and safe practice are paramount throughout, and only you know what is appropriate for the young people in your PE lessons.

Before the lesson

- Where possible, give an indication of what you will be doing before the actual lesson. This can be given in advance, potentially 24 hours, especially if the young person is anxious.
- Ask the young person to contribute to your ideas of inclusion. Empower them.
- Ask the young person if they wish to work with a friend/group for particular activities. Consider doing this discreetly at first if you do not know the young person.
- Ask the young person if they wish for you to share some do's and don'ts to the class about processing information. The young person may wish to lead this but allow them the choice. Create an atmosphere where the class feel comfortable to ask questions about other's particular learning needs a positive, considerate way.
- Consider having Picture Exchange Communication System (PECS) to assist with equipment and order of activities ahead and throughout the session if appropriate. Microsoft Immersive Reader is also useful to change words into pictures.

During the lesson

- Have signs and colours on the wall/fences to help use as reference points for directional sense.
- Always point out and reinforce the direction they are travelling to.
- Provide a list of activities that will be experienced and ask the young person to tick them off as they proceed through the lesson.
- Encourage the young person to ask for clarity if necessary.
- Allow rest breaks if the young person seems anxious.

After the lesson

■ Allow the young person to feedback on what worked well for them.

■ Seek out if the young person felt challenged enough, did their understanding/ability to process information improve?

■ Personally reflect on the suitability of your lesson.

OPEN – everyone can be included with very little modification

■ Send the lesson plan to the teaching assistant and/or young person 24 hours before the lesson.
■ Ask if the young person needs a guide.
■ Break down the instructions and repeat should you need to.

MODIFIED – Using changes to Space, Task, Equipment, People (STEP) to include all

■ Identify the section of map being utilised. Enlarge and colour photocopy. All elements of the map including symbols, footpaths and key landmarks will be enlarged and more recognisable.
■ For longer distances, task small groups to design a visual trail (Appendix B) and allow others to do the same. Swap trails and follow (consider the terrain).
■ Place questions or images as well as coordinates at the points so all young people can contribute in different ways.

Photo 5.4 Using photographs is a useful way to create trails for some young people

(Continued)

PARALLEL – activities delivered simultaneously which allow for different starting points

- Print out a Google Map of school grounds. Allow the young person to set up base in a central location and practise orientating the map.
- The young person should be encouraged to pick out features from the map and navigate their way to them.
- If going on a trail, use photographs of the area that the young person will be navigating around. Trail photograph maps should reflect the route that the young person should follow.
- Each junction (opportunity for the young person to turn right or left) should be identified with annotated photographs to help understanding.

SPECIFIC – purposeful related activity to develop or enhance a skill

- A student can draw their own map and design their own key with colour coding to identify landmarks and features.
- The young person can create a route around their own map and share with others.

DISABILITY – introducing disability-specific sports

Reverse integration
- Photocopy the young person's map and then allow the young people to share their map with the rest of the group. The young person can deliver a competition of who can complete their route the quickest for example.

Additional resources
- There could be an opportunity for you to promote mainstream sport as well as impairment-specific competitive pathways such as the Special Olympics. Try:
- https://www.mencap.org.uk/about-us/what-we-do/mencap-sport
- http://www.uksportsassociation.org/
- https://www.specialolympics.org/

Orienteering for young people who may have difficulty walking or climbing stairs

Key considerations

This list is in no particular order, nor is it essential to complete each and every time. It provides suggestions of *some* of the ways in which you can support the young person in your class. Some may be more relevant than others, so select what may work best for you. Safety and safe practice are paramount throughout, and only you know what is appropriate for the young people in your PE lessons.

Before the lesson

■ Where possible, give an indication of what you will be doing before the actual lesson. This can be given in advance, potentially 24 hours, especially if the young person is anxious.

■ Ask the young person to contribute to your ideas of inclusion. Empower them.

■ Ask the young person if they wish to work with a friend/group for particular activities. Consider doing this discreetly at first if you do not know the young person.

■ Ask the young person if they wish for you to share some do's and don'ts to the class about wheelchair etiquette. The young person may wish to lead this but allow them the choice. Create an atmosphere where the class feel comfortable to ask questions about other's particular learning needs in a positive, considerate way.

■ Consider the terrain and if the area is suitably accessible.

During the lesson

■ If fatigue becomes an issue, allow the young person in a wheelchair to lead and create a flexible rule. However, this should not always be the rule, as the young person needs to be integrated.

■ Allow and encourage pupils to adapt rules to enhance enjoyment and inclusivity themselves.

■ Encourage the young person to ask for clarity if necessary.

■ Allow rest breaks if necessary.

After the lesson

■ Allow the young person to feedback on what worked well for them.

■ Seek out if the young person felt challenged enough, did their cognition improve?

■ Personally reflect on the suitability of your lesson.

(Continued)

OPEN – everyone can be included with very little modification

- Use a resource card including diagrams/photos if necessary.
- Select appropriate location. Consider terrain.
- Ask the young person if they would like the teaching assistant to keep hold of the map for them.
- Discuss with the young person what their range of movements is.

MODIFIED – Using changes to Space, Task, Equipment, People (STEP) to include all

- Select a section of map that will be used. Some woodland areas have designated 'accessible' trails. Ensure that it is easily accessible to the young person.
- Break down the movement and allow repetition of action before moving on.
- Hand draw a map of a small, navigable area, for example, school playground/adventure playground. Use old climbing rope to set up a rope course that is fixed to these features. Using the map, the young person can plot their route through the course and then follow it. The rope being tied to the features will offer a certain level of support for the young person to hold onto and guide their way around the walk without relying on a teaching assistant.

PARALLEL – activities delivered simultaneously which allow for different starting points

- Ask the young person what they feel they can do and allow them to progress with additional challenges each session.
- Create a static activity if necessary, and match flashcards of symbols/features to descriptive words.
- Allow the young person to draw their own version of map and create their own key and colour code. Plot a route on the map and follow.
- Plot a route for someone else to follow – give verbal and/or written instructions.
- Take photographs of an object and plot on the map. Working with a partner send partner to locate object. Can continue the use of technology by getting partner to take picture of the same object if desired.
- For longer distances, task small groups to design a visual trail (Appendix B), and allow others to do the same. Swap trails and follow (consider the terrain).

SPECIFIC – purposeful related activity to develop or enhance a skill

- Complete a trail around the school grounds deciding where **they** want to explore (allow the young person to pick the best route for them). Ask them to lay down cones as they complete the route. Once they are happy with their route, they can draw a map of the area and then plot their route on their personalised map.
- Download the Ordinance Survey map app and allow the young person to practise plotting routes online. Encourage the young person to familiarise themselves with features. In addition, you can give the young person a 'virtual' start and finish point for them to plot different routes to get from start to finish, for example, the quickest route that encompasses most height or a route that passes most water sources.

DISABILITY – introducing disability-specific sports

Reverse integration

■ Photocopy the young person's map and then share their map with the rest of the group. The young person can deliver a competition of who can complete their route the quickest for example.

■ Ask the young person to instruct the group to draw a map of their roped route and then plot a route around it. The young person can encourage the group to make use of equipment if able and confident enough to do so.

Additional resources

https://disabledramblers.co.uk/
https://chairinstitute.com/outdoor-activities-for-wheelchair-users/
https://www.cerebralpalsyguidance.com/cerebral-palsy/living/enjoying-outdoors/
https://www.advenchair.com/

Orienteering for young people who may have difficulty with upper body movement and control

Key considerations

This list is in no particular order, nor is it essential to complete each and every time. It provides suggestions of *some* of the ways in which you can support the young person in your class. Some may be more relevant than others, so select what may work best for you. Safety and safe practice are paramount throughout, and only you know what is appropriate for the young people in your PE lessons.

Before the lesson

■ Where possible, give an indication of what you will be doing before the actual lesson. This can be given in advance, potentially 24 hours, especially if the young person is anxious.

■ Ask the young person to contribute to your ideas of inclusion. Empower them.

■ Ask the young person if they wish to work with a friend/group for particular activities. Consider doing this discreetly at first if you do not know the young person.

■ Ask the young person if they wish for you to share some do's and don'ts to the class about limb movement. The young person may wish to lead this but allow them the choice. Create an atmosphere where the class feel comfortable to ask questions about other's particular learning needs in a positive, considerate way.

(Continued)

- Consider the sports/activities on the curriculum: are there better, more inclusive activities that could be trialled or included?

- Laminate maps in case of bad weather. Paper copies will fray and tear in rain. Laminating will also avoid bends in the map, which, over a few hours, can become unreadable, leading to key features being overlooked.

- Encourage peers to work in consideration of the young person who may have additional needs especially if they can see the young person may be in danger. Specific instructions could be given to one peer to help clarify information given by the teacher to the young person.

- It is valuable to allow all young people to experience working with others outside of their friendship group.

During the lesson

- Be mindful of balance.
- Check in with the young person on their engagement/preference.
- Other body parts may be used instead (if appropriate).
- Encourage the young person to ask for clarity if necessary.
- Allow rest breaks if the young person seems anxious.
- Make sure the young person is being challenged in the activity you have set.

After the lesson

- Allow the young person to feedback on what worked well for them.
- Seek out if the young person felt challenged enough, did their skills improve?
- Personally reflect on the suitability of your lesson.

OPEN – everyone can be included with very little modification

There should be no real reason to adapt the activities in order to include a young person who has difficulty with upper body movement and control. However, it would be helpful to purchase a waterproof map holder with adjustable and safe lanyard, in order to allow the young person to keep the map close to hand without carrying round the route.

The following website might be useful: http://limbpower.com/

Activity 2: Problem-solving/communication skills – chasing the chicken rounders

The concept of this activity is to develop teamwork and the ability to communicate effectively and work cohesively as a group to solve problems. This game can be played in a forest area or school playground/field depending on the group's needs.

Concept of the game

Two groups work as two separate teams. One team throws a toy rubber chicken (dog toys work well for this or other non-hazardous objects) and then forms a tight circle as a group. The thrower then completes laps around the group in order to score a rounder, whilst the other group retrieves the toy rubber chicken and passes under the legs of all their group members. The quicker they pass under their legs, the sooner they prevent the other team from scoring rounders. The team that have just passed under their legs then become the 'batting team'. Repeat. Each complete lap = 1 point/rounder. Encourage the groups to think tactically when they are 'batting' and when they are fielding, in order to outwit their opponents. How can they work more effectively together as a team?

Points to consider

- When using markers, consider spot mats or coloured chalk boldly marked to outline the area, instead of cones to avoid tripping hazards.

- Devise hands-up method when play has stopped, so that young people who may not hear well are aware the game has stopped.

- Be aware of noise levels within the group, as when playing this may cause unnecessary stress.

- Important to check with the young person as to what they feel their movement capacity is before commencement of the activity.

- Allow the young person to guide you as to how they feel they can integrate themselves within the game.

Problem-solving/communication skills for young people who may have difficulty seeing, even when wearing glasses

OPEN – everyone can be included with very little modification

- Ask if a player can narrate the activity as they play to help with understanding and game awareness.

MODIFIED – Using changes to Space, Task, Equipment, People (STEP) to include all

- Show the young person the selection of rubber toys or other non-hazardous throwing implements. Can use much larger, much brighter toys if required. Allow the young person to select the preferred 'throwing' object.
- Select a toy with noise, for example, vortex ball to help with the direction of travel.
- Section off an area and explain to all young people that this is a safe running channel/area for the young person.

PARALLEL – activities delivered simultaneously which allow for different starting points

- Potentially, identify the young person as a chief thrower. The group can score more points depending on how quickly they return the toy rubber chicken to the young person.
- Work in a small group to identify the range of key audio cues to help locate the object and gradually increase the speed in which the object is identified.
- Identify two groups. Both complete the same activity and follow the same rules, but one group competes at a walking pace and the other group competes at running. The young person can select which group they wish to join.

SPECIFIC – purposeful related activity to develop or enhance a skill

- Use range of various size and shape objects that the young person can grasp and throw.
- Practise throwing vortex ball and using specific commands from the partner to locate the object.
- Use voice to give direction.
- Walk the student around the area (if needed).

DISABILITY – introducing disability-specific sports

Reverse integration
- The young person can devise new rules based on the use of new equipment and teach the adapted version of the game to the rest of the class.

Additional resources
- See the previous section, titled 'Activity 1: Problem-Solving – Map Reading and Navigation Skills'.

Problem-solving/communication skills for young people who may have hearing difficulty, even when using a hearing aid. This can also incorporate linguistic difficulties

OPEN – everyone can be included with very little modification

- If applicable, provide visual resource cards that the young person can refer to throughout the lesson.
- Ask if they want a buddy to work with to verify/explain the teacher's instructions.
- Make sure the class are aware of how to attract the attention of the young person.
- Make sure the pupils face the young person (if the young person reads lips).

MODIFIED – Using changes to Space, Task, Equipment, People (STEP) to include all

- Select one person only to count the rounder's scores on each team to keep noise levels to a minimum.
- Change focus of the game to develop non-verbal communication and encourage the group to work as a team to decide on ways in which they can succeed using non-verbal cues only, such as waving and hand signals.
- Split class into smaller groups and allow them to work with classmates they feel comfortable with if required.

PARALLEL – activities delivered simultaneously which allow for different starting points

- Work in a small group to identify the range of non-verbal communication skills to help locate the object and gradually increase the speed in which the object is identified.
- Identify two groups. Both complete the same activity and follow the same rules, but one group competes at a walking pace and the other group competes at running. The young person can select which group they wish to join.

SPECIFIC – purposeful related activity to develop or enhance a skill

There should be no need to separate the young person. However, if balance is problematic, the young person can develop movement skills and balance by throwing and collecting the object against a clock. The aim is to beat the time set. The young person can integrate into the main session when they feel competent.

DISABILITY – introducing disability-specific sports

Reverse integration
- The young person can devise new rules based on any rule changes implemented during modification stage and teach the adapted version of the game to the rest of the class.

Additional resources
- See the previous section titled 'Activity 1: Problem-Solving – Map Reading and Navigation Skills'.

Problem solving/communication skills for young people who may have difficulty remembering or concentrating

OPEN – everyone can be included with very little modification

- Send the lesson plan to the teaching assistant and/or young person 24 hours before the lesson.
- Ask if the young person needs a guide.
- Use a resource card including diagrams/photos if necessary.
- Repeat instructions, should you need to.
- Ask a peer to propel the toy rubber chicken if appropriate.

MODIFIED – Using changes to Space, Task, Equipment, People (STEP) to include all

- Create a safe channel should the young person need it and explain this area to classmates.
- Adapt equipment to include the use of throwing object with unusual texture to help grasp the ball – for example, puffer ball or Koosh ball.
- Use visual cues to assist with understanding.

PARALLEL – activities delivered simultaneously which allow for different starting points

- The young person can contribute to team points (rounders) by throwing objects into set locations or distances. Can work by themselves in a pair or within the main group(s).
- Break down different elements of the game so experience is gained in isolation first.

SPECIFIC – purposeful related activity to develop or enhance a skill

- Use instruction sheets for teaching assistants so they can engage the young person if they go off-task or misinterpret the activity.

DISABILITY – introducing disability-specific sports

Reverse integration
- The young person can devise new rules based on the use of new equipment and teach the adapted version of the game to the rest of the class.

Additional resources
- See the previous section titled 'Activity 1: Problem-Solving – Map Reading and Navigation Skills'.

Problem-solving activities/communications skills for young people who may have difficulty walking or climbing stairs

OPEN – everyone can be included with very little modification

- Make others in the class stand with their back towards the thrower so they are delayed in seeing the flight of the toy rubber chicken.
- Select an appropriate location. Consider terrain.
- Consider pupils moving towards the young person to lessen travel.
- If travel is key, then provide a range of distances to suit ability and allow choice.
- Choose a static activity but with vigorous use of arms (if applicable) to raise the heart rate.
- Break down the movement and allow the repetition of action before moving on.

MODIFIED – Using changes to Space, Task, Equipment, People (STEP) to include all

- Consider the initial area. School playground/sports hall is more appropriate for manual wheelchair or walker.
- Section off an area of space close to the activity so that wheelchairs or walkers can move freely. If the young person wishes to work away from the rest of the group, then they could be encouraged to decide how they could score a rounder and contribute to the overall team score.
- Over time as the class get used to moving around or to the wheelchair or walker, and the young person with the wheelchair/walker gets more confident, allow integration by implementing designated scoring squares that participants can run to or peers run to where the person with limited movement is situated.
- As above, communicate with the young person in wheelchair/walker about the control/pace of chair. Start with a larger space and generally narrow it down and integrate if possible and safe.
- Adapt equipment to include the use of throwing object with unusual texture to help grasp the ball – for example, puffer ball or Koosh ball if required. Or use a sensory ball on stick so student can choose whether to hold ball or narrow stick attached to the ball, should grasping object be an issue, or use a tactile sensory ring for easier grip.
- Could create a team tag game where the young person in the powerchair tells them what direction to throw/hit and their partner propels it.
- Place the throwing object on a static tee so as to not compromise the balance of the young person.
- Allow the young person to take the role of chief thrower.
- Choose a suitable playing surface such as playground that is flat rather than forest floor.
- Rather than gathering around the thrower to score rounders, a separate group could play a modified version where the team all run/walk to touch an object (e.g. tree) or around a coned area to score a set amount of designated points for their team rather than individual rounders. Can have several designated areas to avoid congestion to score points rather than rounders. Designated areas can vary in distance and size so there is always a closer option if wheelchairs are required.
- The young person can contribute to team points (rounders) by throwing objects into set locations or distances. Can work by themselves in a pair or within the main group(s).

(Continued)

PARALLEL – activities delivered simultaneously which allow for different starting points

- The options in the modified section above may serve as a more inclusive activity, but skills can be broken down into parallel activities if necessary and desired.

SPECIFIC – purposeful related activity to develop or enhance a skill

- Place items on top of a skittle for the young person to practise knocking off/hitting.
- Partner work to practise throwing and retrieving. Wheelchair user knocks the object off the skittle; the partner retrieves and returns to wheelchair user. Both have to get to the designated area to score points.
- Practise knocking the object from the tee. Exploring ways to generate more power to make the object travel further.
- Use an oversized inflatable football that can be moved by using a powerchair. Set targets to aim for and allocate points per target area. The young person may like to reintegrate into the session; once they feel confident, they can move the object.
- Practise throwing first for confidence before integration into an activity.
- Practise throwing and then moving to a different area to replicate how to score a rounder.
- Allow the young person to build in opposite hand to opposite leg when throwing an object.
- Working with a teaching assistant or partner, practise throwing or kicking an object into a pre-identified area.
- Create a range of areas for the young person to aim to help contribute to the number of rounders their team can score. Alter the size and distance of targets to challenge the young person.

DISABILITY – introducing disability-specific sports

Reverse integration

- The young person can teach inclusive rounders to the rest of the group.
- The young person can organise a mini tournament with two tiers: walking group and running group. The young person can identify rules and equipment that must be used and can be creative with how pupils communicate: verbally or non-verbally.
- The young person can teach the game based on scoring rounders in designated areas.

Additional resources

- See the previous section titled 'Activity 1: Problem-Solving – Map Reading and Navigation Skills'.

Problem-solving/communication skills for young people who may have difficulty with upper body movement and control

OPEN – everyone can be included with very little modification

- Discuss with the student what their range of movements is and amend if necessary.
- Use an item to propel the toy rubber chicken or other objects that will travel easily.

MODIFIED – Using changes to Space, Task, Equipment, People (STEP) to include all

- Select an object that can be kicked instead. Oversized football would work well.
- Stop the opposition from scoring rounders by everyone touching the object with their feet rather than passing under the legs.

PARALLEL – activities delivered simultaneously which allow for different starting points

- Can make the young person the central point for scoring rounders to minimise the movement. Additionally, the young person can move to a set scoring 'zone'.

SPECIFIC – purposeful related activity to develop or enhance a skill

- Should not need to separate the young person, however, you may want to in order to:
  - Practise kicking first for confidence before integration into activity.
  - Practise kicking and then moving to a different area to replicate how to score a rounder.

DISABILITY – introducing disability-specific sports

Reverse integration

The young person can organise a mini tournament with two tiers: walking group and running group. The young person can identify rules and equipment that must be used and can be creative with how pupils communicate, verbally or non-verbally.

Additional resources

- See the previous section titled 'Activity 1: Problem-Solving – Map Reading and Navigation Skills'.

Activity 3: Team building – giants, wizards and elves

This activity is best used as a warm-up to teach teambuilding. It encourages communication and working together to beat opponents. Depending on which activity type you are leading, you will need to consider location. A flat, even surface area/floor space would be more desirable in most instances. This activity is largely based on physical actions rather than words.

Points to consider:

■ As the teacher, when starting the chain of 'giants, wizards and elves', and when the two groups meet for the first time, use non-verbal hand signals, such as arm raised for quiet and arm dropped down to initiate the start of the activity.

■ Allow the young person to work at the end of the line so they do not feel enclosed by the group and can step out if required.

■ Consider a terrain/playing area for ease of movement.

Concept of game

This game is a variation of traditional rock, paper, scissors game:

■ Giants can trample elves.

■ Elves can trip up wizards.

■ Wizards can zap giants!

Use the following actions:

■ Giants = big hands raised above head and roar!

■ Wizards = sideward stance and point a pretend wand!

■ Elves = squat to floor and make yourself smaller.

Each group decides what they want to be: giants, wizards or elves. Give the group 20 seconds to decide. Starting 10m apart, they then turn and walk towards each other. When you call out 'giants, wizards, or elves', the class perform their chosen actions. Depending on the outcome, they will either retreat or attack; for example, giants will chase elves, but elves can chase wizards. If a player gets tagged when retreating, they have to join the other team. Whoever has the most players in their team at the end is the winning team.

Photo 5.5 Include activities that encourage self-expression and creativity

Team building for young people who may have difficulty seeing, even when wearing glasses

OPEN – everyone can be included with very little modification

- If required, have a teaching assistant working directly with the young person to reiterate actions required for giants, wizards and elves. Ensure the teaching assistant has asked the young person if they understand the movements required for each action by using open questions.
- Mirror the moves so the young person can copy them. Additionally, you might gently manually put the young person in the position of the giants, wizards, and elves if they are happy for you to do so, whilst verbally explaining.

MODIFIED – Using changes to Space, Task, Equipment, People (STEP) to include all

- Make the active area smaller.
- Place opposing teams in bright coloured bibs to allow the young person to view team walking towards and moving away from them.

PARALLEL – activities delivered simultaneously which allow for different starting points

- Split the class into smaller groups and have a walking, jogging, skipping, hopping, or sprinting group that the young person can work within.

SPECIFIC – purposeful related activity to develop or enhance a skill

- The young person works with the teaching assistant or partner initially to rehearse movements required until confident and can then integrate at any point. The young person learns at own pace and only joins the session when they feel ready.

(Continued)

DISABILITY – introducing disability-specific sports

Reverse integration
- The young person can lead the session where each person in the group pairs up with a buddy, one person in the pair is blindfolded and their buddy has to guide them. This will give the young person a heightened sense of what it is like with limited vision, as well as developing effective team work and communication skills.

Additional resources
- See the previous section titled 'Activity 1: Problem-Solving – Map Reading and Navigation Skills'.

Team building for young people who may have hearing difficulty, even when using a hearing aid. This can also incorporate linguistic difficulties

OPEN – everyone can be included with very little modification

- Ensure the group is quiet at the start.

MODIFIED – Using changes to Space, Task, Equipment, People (STEP) to include all

- Allow the young person to decide which character they will be each time. By placing the ownership on the young person the rest of the class will have to listen carefully and ensure quiet to be able to hear command given.

PARALLEL – activities delivered simultaneously which allow for different starting points

- Split the class into smaller groups and have a walking group which the young person can work within.
- Place certain emphasis on actions such as 'slow motion' and encourage groups to 'act' actions out as exaggerated as possible.

SPECIFIC – purposeful related activity to develop or enhance a skill

- The young person reviews resource card images and practises actions.

DISABILITY – introducing disability-specific sports

Reverse integration
- The young person can make up a new set of actions that can beat each other and teach the group their version – could be, for example, three hand signals.

Additional resources
- See the previous section titled 'Activity 1: Problem-Solving – Map Reading and Navigation Skills'.

Team building for young people who may have difficulty remembering or concentrating

OPEN – everyone can be included with very little modification

- Send the lesson plan to the teaching assistant and/or young person before the lesson.
- Ask if the young person needs a buddy.
- Use a resource card including diagrams/photos of the three concepts: giants, wizards and elves.
- Repeat instructions, should you need to.

MODIFIED – Using changes to Space, Task, Equipment, People (STEP) to include all

- Create a safe channel should the young person need it and explain this area to classmates.

PARALLEL – activities delivered simultaneously which allow for different starting points

- Smaller groups, pairs or fours.
- Can practise actions and tally points scored instead of chasing each other to win members for their team.

SPECIFIC – purposeful related activity to develop or enhance a skill

- Paired work – rock, paper, scissors, etc. (it is more likely they will be familiar with this concept).
- Progress to new actions using visual resource cards if appropriate and practise actions of giants, wizards and elves.
- Once confident with actions, students can then chase each other depending on the outcome of action.
- This should allow gradual integration into the group.

DISABILITY – introducing disability-specific sports

Additional resources
- See the previous section titled 'Activity 1: Problem-Solving – Map Reading and Navigation Skills'.

Team building for young people who may have difficulty walking or climbing stairs

OPEN – everyone can be included with very little modification

- Use a resource card including diagrams/photos if necessary.
- Check that the young person understands the concept of the game by asking open-ended questions.
- Allow the young person to have a buddy if they wish.
- Break down the movements and allow the repetition of action before moving on.
- Use a resource card including diagrams/photos if necessary.

(Continued)

MODIFIED – Using changes to Space, Task, Equipment, People (STEP) to include all

- Select a playground area.
- Split the class into smaller groups to avoid classmates running into wheelchairs.
- Give the group a specific command to carry out actions – for example, slow motion and award additional point for best acting out of actions to encourage cooperation and team work and take emphasis away from point scoring and competition.
- Can perform actions statically to allow the young person to maintain balance.
- Split the class into smaller groups.

PARALLEL – activities delivered simultaneously which allow for different starting points

- Practise actions with the teaching assistant/partner using a visual resource card if necessary.
- Integrate back into a group once the young person and teacher are happy with actions.
- Split the class into smaller groups and have a walking group which the young person can work within.
- Place certain emphasis on actions such as 'slow motion' and encourage groups to 'act' actions out as exaggerated as possible.
- Smaller groups, pairs or fours practise actions and tally points scored instead of chasing each other to win members for their team.

SPECIFIC – purposeful related activity to develop or enhance a skill

- As above.
- Perform wheelchair movements that reflect giants, wizards and elves… try and outsmart partner or teaching assistant.
- The young person can be given time to create movements and then explain why they are, what they are and what they mean. Points scored for every time they successfully outwit their partner.
- Can have large chalk diagrams or writing on the floor (tarmac). The student must go to the picture they wish to. Their partner will then hold up the picture they selected, and whoever wins obtains the points.
- Young people could work with a teaching assistant or buddy to identify three items from nature that all have 'special' powers. Students can then use these to play against one another.

DISABILITY – introducing disability-specific sports

Reverse integration
- Can lead one group by making decisions as to which character they will be.
- Generate group discussion as to why characters have been selected (problem-solving).
- The young person can make up a new set of actions that can beat each other and teach the group their version – could be, for example, three hand signals.
- The young person can teach the adapted version of the games based on the items they have found and the roles they have created from nature.

Additional resources
- See the previous section titled 'Activity 1: Problem-Solving – Map Reading and Navigation Skills'.

Team building for young people who may have difficulty with upper body movement and control

OPEN – everyone can be included with very little modification

- Use a resource card including diagrams/photos if necessary.
- Check that the young person understands the concept of the game by asking open-ended questions.
- Allow the young person to have a buddy if they wish.
- Adapt the actions if necessary.
- Use a resource card including diagrams/photos if necessary.

MODIFIED – Using changes to Space, Task, Equipment, People (STEP) to include all

- Split the class into smaller groups.

PARALLEL – activities delivered simultaneously which allow for different starting points

- In small groups, allow them to create their own ideas that minimise upper body movements. Provide specific instructions such as; all actions must be from below waist height, for example, standing with legs apart.

SPECIFIC – purposeful related activity to develop or enhance a skill

- Should not need to have a separate activity.

DISABILITY – introducing disability-specific sports

Reverse integration
- The young person can make up a new set of actions that can beat each other and teach the group their version – could be, for example, three hand signals.

Additional resources
- See the previous section titled 'Activity I: Problem-Solving – Map Reading and Navigation Skills'.

Activity 4: Cooperation and trust – rope of peace

This activity is best used as a warm-up to teaching team building. It encourages communication and working together to achieve an outcome. Use a hands-up approach, so the whole class knows when to be quiet and help alert the young person to the fact that the session may be changing/moving on.

Concept of the game

The group forms a circle and holds a rope in their hands pulling the rope to create tension. As a group they use the rope to kneel down without losing their balance and then all stand up again together. Each individual must allow and trust the rope to take their weight.

Photo 5.6 Teamwork activities sometimes allow others to shine in different ways

Points to consider

- Requires a good level of core body strength.

Cooperation and trust activities for young people who may have difficulty seeing, even when wearing glasses

OPEN – everyone can be included with very little modification

■ Ask the young person if they would like the teaching assistant to work directly in front of them for assistance.

MODIFIED – Using changes to Space, Task, Equipment, People (STEP) to include all

■ Use a thicker rope so the student can feel that the rope is secure and strong enough.

PARALLEL – activities delivered simultaneously which allow for different starting points

■ In pairs use a skipping rope (knotted) and practise as a pair. Develop trust and confidence in a smaller group to start with.
■ Practise kneeling and standing holding someone else's hands instead of a rope.

SPECIFIC – purposeful related activity to develop or enhance a skill

■ The young person can practise leaning against wall, leaning back and kneeling with weight against wall to increase confidence and awareness.

DISABILITY – introducing disability-specific sports

Reverse integration
■ The young person can teach the activity with a new rule where everyone must wear a blindfold.

Additional resources
■ See the previous section titled 'Activity 1: Problem-Solving – Map Reading and Navigation Skills'.

Cooperation and trust activities for young people who may have hearing difficulty, even when using a hearing aid. This can also incorporate linguistic difficulties

OPEN – everyone can be included with very little modification

■ Share visual aid with the young person to demonstrate the activity, rules and guidelines.
■ Ask the young person if they would like to work with a peer/partner with whom they feel confident.

MODIFIED – Using changes to Space, Task, Equipment, People (STEP) to include all

■ Students can complete the task in silence. Work as a group to develop non-verbal communication skills.

(Continued)

PARALLEL – activities delivered simultaneously which allow for different starting points

- In pairs use a skipping rope (knotted) and practise as a pair. Develop trust and confidence in a smaller group to start with.
- Practise kneeling and standing holding someone else's hands instead of a rope.

SPECIFIC – purposeful related activity to develop or enhance a skill

- As above.

DISABILITY – introducing disability-specific sports

Additional resources

- See the previous section titled 'Activity 1: Problem-Solving – Map Reading and Navigation Skills'.

Cooperation and trust activities for young people who may have difficulty remembering or concentrating

OPEN – everyone can be included with very little modification

- Break down the movements and allow the repetition of action before moving on.
- Check whether the young person understands the concept of the game by asking open-ended questions.
- Allow the young person to have a partner if they wish.

MODIFIED – Using changes to Space, Task, Equipment, People (STEP) to include all

- Elements of the activity that can be changed include:
  - o Different types of communication such as verbal or non-verbal.
  - o Identify set leaders within the group.
  - o Blindfold some students for additional challenge.

PARALLEL – activities delivered simultaneously which allow for different starting points

- Use a resource card including diagrams/photos, if necessary, to understand concept.
- Break down the activity. Allow the young person to work with a partner on basic trust exercises, for example, standing back to back and crouching down putting your weight against each other to maintain balance.

SPECIFIC – purposeful related activity to develop or enhance a skill

- Practise holding a skipping rope at one end with the teaching assistant/partner at other and familiarise self with pulling on the rope to take the body weight.
- Encourage the teaching assistant to allow more or less force depending on confidence of the young person.

DISABILITY – introducing disability-specific sports

Reverse integration

■ The young person can lead discussion with the group about the important aspects of how to communicate effectively with them. What is important when communicating with the young person with learning/cognitive impairment? What skills could they learn to be better communicators?

Additional resources

■ See the previous section titled 'Activity I: Problem-Solving – Map Reading and Navigation Skills'.

Cooperation and trust activities for young people who may have difficulty walking or climbing stairs

OPEN – everyone can be included with very little modification

■ Use a resource card including diagrams/photos if necessary.
■ Ask the young person if they would like to work with a buddy whom they feel confident with.

MODIFIED – Using changes to Space, Task, Equipment, People (STEP) to include all

■ Apply and maintain tension on the rope from a static position to contribute to team success.
■ Place the rope around the back of the chair so that the young person feels included and is able to contribute to tension with the rope make sure brakes are applied.
■ If the young person feels uncomfortable with the rope around the back of the chair, ask them to guide the wheels onto the rope and apply the brake in order to help the group maintain tension. This could also be done with the whole class sitting down. They all have to pull the rope taught and lean back. If they work successfully as a team, they should be able to use the rope to lean back and pull themselves back up to a sitting position.
■ Elements of the activity that can be changed include the following:
   o Level of communication (verbal/non-verbal).
   o Identify set leaders within the group.
   o Blindfold some students for additional challenge.
   o Students can have a 'spotter' (which is another young person who stands behind them and is ready to guide/support if required).

PARALLEL – activities delivered simultaneously which allow for different starting points

■ Place the rope underneath the wheelchair in between front and back wheels. Working with a partner who is at the opposite end of the rope, ask the partner to start from a sitting position and gently use the rope to lean back. The tension provided from the wheelchair should allow the partner to lean all the way back and then sit back up again.
■ The young person can practise leaning against wall, leaning back and kneeling with weight against wall to increase confidence and awareness.

(Continued)

SPECIFIC – purposeful related activity to develop or enhance a skill

- Guiding the young person over the rope and securing the rope with their wheels can be made into a task itself, where the group can give specific signals, verbally or non-verbally to get the young person in the correct place.
- Holding a skipping rope (seated) at one end with teaching assistant/partner at the other end, the young person familiarises themselves with someone pulling on the rope to take the body weight.
- The teaching assistant can allow more or less force depending on confidence of the young person.
- Practise taking weight on a skipping rope with someone sensible at the other end, for example, teaching assistant. The teaching assistant can adjust how much force they put through the rope to see how hard the young person has to pull to make some movements.
- Lay out some zones that equate to points, and if they can pull their partner into the zones, they accrue points for their team.

DISABILITY – introducing disability-specific sports

Reverse integration

- The young person can lead discussion with the group about the important aspects of how to communicate effectively with them. What is important when communicating with the young person with a physical impairment? What skills could they learn to be better communicators?

Additional resources

- See the previous section titled 'Activity 1: Problem-Solving – Map Reading and Navigation Skills'.

Cooperation and trust activities for young people who may have difficulty with upper body movement and control

OPEN – everyone can be included with very little modification

- Share visual aid with the young person to demonstrate the activity, rules and guidelines.
- Check whether the young person understands the concept of the game by asking open-ended questions.
- Allow the young person to have a buddy if they wish.

MODIFIED – Using changes to Space, Task, Equipment, People (STEP) to include all

- The young person can have input into how they feel about contributing to the group task of applying tension to the rope, for example, sitting on it, standing on it, lying on it, etc. They may be able to simply form an anchor point on the rope without putting any weight through it.

PARALLEL – activities delivered simultaneously which allow for different starting points

- Tie two skipping ropes together and allow the young person to sit with the rope on the floor behind them, but use hands (if appropriate) to hold onto knots in the rope. This will help them to grasp the rope. Meanwhile a partner can sit at the other end of the skipping rope and use the tension created from the young person to lean back using the rope. The partner will also need to be sitting down to avoid the rope riding up the young person's back.

SPECIFIC – purposeful related activity to develop or enhance a skill

- The teaching assistant can allow more or less force depending on confidence of the young person.

DISABILITY – introducing disability-specific sports

Reverse integration
- Restrict other people's body parts in the formulation of the task.

Additional resources
- See the previous section titled 'Activity 1: Problem-Solving – Map Reading and Navigation Skills'.

Activity 5 – Balloon balance

This activity is best used as a warm-up to teach team building. It encourages communication and working together to achieve an outcome. The activity may be best placed indoors to avoid balloons blowing away. To create a heavier balloon ball, dry rice can be added to weigh the balloon down slightly. If you only have an outdoor space, use soft objects that are less likely to roll away. Consider the positioning of group/s and ensure the area is not too busy and crowded as to minimise background noise for the young person. If appropriate, allow the young person to work in a quiet space to be able to focus on the task. Some young people may not like the feel of the balloons, so consider balloon balls that have a cloth coating or a lighter paper ball. Some young people may have an aversion to latex (the texture, the noise if it bursts), so check before the activity is undertaken.

Concept of the game

How many balloons can be used in the group at once? All balloons must be off the floor and touching somebody/something.

Teamwork for young people who may have difficulty seeing, even when wearing glasses

OPEN – everyone can be included with very little modification

- Ask the young person if they would like a buddy/guide to help direct them through the activity.

MODIFIED – Using changes to Space, Task, Equipment, People (STEP) to include all

- Use jumbo balloons.
- Use brightly/bold coloured balloons.
- Tether the balloons to a weight so the young person can still move freely, but if the balloons drop to the floor, they will stay within the general area that the young person is working.

PARALLEL – activities delivered simultaneously which allow for different starting points

- Working in pairs, practise trapping balloons between various body parts.
- Specify challenges; for example, trap one balloon between your arms, legs, feet, etc.

SPECIFIC – purposeful related activity to develop or enhance a skill

- Allow the young person to creatively come up with ways to trap balloons by themselves.
- Share ideas with the group with regard to new ideas of how to trap the balloon.

DISABILITY – introducing disability-specific sports

Reverse integration

■ Blindfold the group playing the same activity. Listen and reflect on the communication skills and thoughts/feelings of the experience and how they may have worked well.

Additional resources

■ See the previous section titled 'Activity 1: Problem-Solving – Map Reading and Navigation Skills'.

Teamwork for young people who may have hearing difficulty, even when using a hearing aid. This can also incorporate linguistic difficulties

OPEN – everyone can be included with very little modification

■ Share visual aid with the young person to demonstrate the activity, rules and guidelines.
■ Ask the young person if they would like to work with a buddy to improve confidence.

MODIFIED – Using changes to Space, Task, Equipment, People (STEP) to include all

■ Set activity areas that the group must stay within. Keep groups apart to keep the noise level and background noise to a minimum.

PARALLEL – activities delivered simultaneously which allow for different starting points

■ Practise using a static object/feature initially, for example, a wall.
■ Practise in pairs to increase confidence and familiarisation with the task.

SPECIFIC – purposeful related activity to develop or enhance a skill

■ Should not need a Specific activity as the young person should be able to take part with everyone else.

DISABILITY – introducing disability-specific sports

Reverse integration

■ Use the young person to facilitate a discussion about how the group can work better together as a team, for example, communication, cooperation and leadership.

Additional resources

■ See the previous section titled 'Activity 1: Problem-Solving – Map Reading and Navigation Skills'.

(Continued)

Teamwork for young people who may have difficulty remembering or concentrating

OPEN – everyone can be included with very little modification

- Break down the activity and allow the repetition of action before moving on.
- Check whether the young person understands the concept of the game by asking open-ended questions.
- Allow the young person to have a buddy if they wish.

MODIFIED – Using changes to Space, Task, Equipment, People (STEP) to include all

- Use a range of equipment that varies in size, texture and weight.

PARALLEL – activities delivered simultaneously which allow for different starting points

- See previous suggestions for Parallel activities.

SPECIFIC – purposeful related activity to develop or enhance a skill

- If the young person does not like physical contact, allow them to see how many balloons they can trap using their own body parts.
- The young person could use a balloon ball or different items to help with their engagement.

DISABILITY – introducing disability-specific sports

Additional resources

- See the previous section titled 'Activity 1: Problem-Solving – Map Reading and Navigation Skills'.
- Share ideas with group with regards to new ideas of how to trap the balloon.

Teamwork for young people who may have difficulty walking or climbing stairs

OPEN – everyone can be included with very little modification

■ Allow the young person to work with a peer.

MODIFIED – Using changes to Space, Task, Equipment, People (STEP) to include all

■ Tether the balloons to a weight so the young person can still move freely. If you are able to work with helium balloons, then this would allow the young person to pick the balloon up with ease as the tether will allow the balloon to stand at an appropriate height.
■ Complete the task sitting down in a small group circle/pairs. See how many balloons can be kept on the floor between them.
■ Vary the weight, size and texture of the objects to allow the young person to grasp and trap in a range of different places either working by themselves or with a partner/small group.

PARALLEL – activities delivered simultaneously which allow for different starting points

■ Working in a small group, they can see how many balloons can be touching the wheelchair at once.
■ Complete sitting or standing (allow the young person the choice); focus of the activity can change slightly to see how long the young person can keep a balloon off the ground.
■ Introduce a second balloon to challenge the young person.
■ Working with a partner, encourage the young person to keep one balloon off the ground with their partner. Gradually introduce more balloons, but discuss ideas with the young person and where they think they can trap a balloon with their partner.

SPECIFIC – purposeful related activity to develop or enhance a skill

■ Student can practise holding object between the wheelchair and static feature such as wall.
■ See how many objects the young person can trap using their own body parts. Vary the shape, size and texture of the object.

DISABILITY – introducing disability-specific sports

Additional resources
■ See the previous section titled 'Activity 1: Problem-Solving – Map Reading and Navigation Skills'.

Teamwork for young people who may have difficulty with upper body movement and control

OPEN – everyone can be included with very little modification

- Check whether the young person understands the concept of the game by asking open-ended questions.
- Allow the young person to have a buddy if they wish.

MODIFIED – Using changes to Space, Task, Equipment, People (STEP) to include all

- Group to sit down in circle and see if they can balance a balloon between every person. Can increase the number of balloons based on the success rate.

PARALLEL – activities delivered simultaneously which allow for different starting points

- Practise trapping a balloon between the young person and a stationary object, for example, a wall.

SEPARATE purposeful related activity to develop or enhance a skill

- See how many balloons they can hold off the ground using their own body to trap the balloons. Each balloon can contribute points to the overall team score.

DISABILITY – introducing disability-specific sports

Additional resources

- See the previous section, titled 'Activity 1: Problem-Solving – Map Reading and Navigation Skills'.

6 Swimming

Kimberley Mortimer, Helen Hope and Rebecca Foster

This chapter has been broken into two parts. The first section looks at generic information for most fundamental swimming skills. The second section introduces aspects for more advanced swimming skills and techniques.

As Physical Education (PE) practitioners your adherence to health, safety and risk remains high within this activity area. PE/swimming teachers receive specific training to be able to teach this activity, and therefore, safety standards, risk assessments, etc. must be understood and applied *before* commencing any of the following activities, and maintained throughout any swimming teaching session.

Teaching progressions for swimming that are used within a mainstream class should remain the same. However, this section provides hints and tips about how to help young people that may need additional/different support, whilst getting to and into the water. The class teacher, swimming instructor, teaching assistant and/or a peer can provide this support.

Aspects will need to be considered pre-lesson time, for instance a young person who may need assistance in seeing even with glasses may have to orientate themselves in the changing rooms prior to the swimming lesson. A young person who has difficulty concentrating or remembering may need to observe the first lesson before participating to comprehend what

Photo 6.1 A young person demonstrating the arm technique of front crawl

Photo 6.2 Using floats to help gain water confidence

they may be expected to do. A teaching assistant would be ideal for this pre-lesson orientation, particularly if they were able to provide a verbal commentary about what was going on, whilst pointing out or mentioning key aspects that may be of interest or importance to the young person. Explanations of textures that the young person may come into contact with through being bare foot and highlighting the importance of holding onto hand rails and pool gutters when in the water are also important aspects to cover prior to the actual lesson taking place. This can also be done pictorially using Picture Exchange Communication System (PECS). These are images (photos, drawings or pictures) of the activities you want the young person to perform in a certain order, or perhaps an order of the activities presented in a lesson. Young people can then follow where they are in the lesson. Some other students may prefer a checklist that they can tick off as you go through the lesson to help them process the time with you. Smells, sounds and lighting may also distress some young people, so consider how the young person may be introduced to the swimming pool environment.

When in the water consider that the young person in question may need to have a separate space in order to orientate themselves within the pool whilst a more formal teaching session is taking place alongside. This may have to be explained to their peers so the group can understand that learning takes place in different forms. Explain to students that adjustments need to be made for each of them to make sure they are safe; therefore, some young people may be allowed to wear goggles or use floats to assist them.

The main teacher/swimming instructor must always remain on the pool side. However, a teaching assistant who is happy to be in the water with students who may need additional support will be a huge benefit for most young people. The access of someone close will be extremely comforting in the early stages of confidence building for those students who are anxious of water. As confidence grows and skill level develops, it is hoped that the teaching assistant will have a less dominant role and can reduce the amount of contact time/support within the water.

Photo 6.3 Having a teaching assistant in the water can support young people who may be anxious

Key considerations before, during and after swimming

This section includes generic advice and guidance that is appropriate for all young people with a disability. Much of the guidance here is also applicable for complete beginners.

Entry into the pool

■ Agree on the preferred communication method to ensure the young person feels safe through the transition to and into the pool. Good eye contact and hand gestures if appropriate aid discussion. If the young person has trouble hearing even when wearing hearing aids, then make sure you are aware of how to get their attention in an emergency. Hearing aids should be removed and kept away from moisture. If the young person is reliant on a hearing device, removal is likely to cause anxiety. The young person may need access to their hearing device if they are nervous and they must feel reassured that they will be looked after appropriately by you or someone they trust. If a young person has a cochlear implant, you will need to seek advice from parents.

■ Set the scene so the young person knows there may be noise and splashing. Explain that water may go into their eyes, but if they wipe the water away, it may be more comfortable.

■ Explain that the acoustics in the pool are unlike a sports hall or classroom, and that the lighting around the pool will be different. That the young person may experience different smells (chlorine).

■ Explain that the young person will have to walk barefoot on a textured (sometimes slippery) surface. Consider getting their feet wet prior to entry to the poolside.

■ Explain about poolside safety issues and how to be safe once in the water, for example closed mouth and roll onto back if possible.

■ Functional ability of the young person needs to be understood by the teacher and teaching assistant.

■ Identify the depth of water and the technique of entry before it is performed. This should be discussed with the young person and refer to their Education Health Care Plan for the correct technique on supporting the young person into the pool. If no assistance is necessary, then use steps or an incline (if possible), a seated or swivel entry may also be a possible alternative for entry into the pool.

■ Reassure those with a short stature that there will be a block in the water to stand on for respite.

■ Allow the young person to have a peer who will perform the entry technique before them and act as a lead when in the water.

■ Suggest an assistant to aid walking along poolside and into water – whilst in the pool walk in front of the young person to provide support and be ready to walk to the side to ensure a safe entry/exit.

■ Make sure the young person knows that the teaching assistant may have to touch their body to support them. Check that the young person is aware and agrees to this and the teaching assistant states where on their body they may make contact with them.

■ Verbal instruction and encouragement should be given throughout.

■ Indicate that the handrails into the pool are smooth to touch, so a firm grip will be needed. These may also be cold to the touch, which may affect the young person.

■ Allow the young person to wear goggles if necessary.

Photo 6.4 Young people need to be made aware that handrails may be cold and slippery before the young person attempts to enter the pool

Anxiety

- Anxiety will be a natural response for some young people; reassure and do not force the young person.

- Allow them to observe the group if they prefer, until they feel more confident.

- Point out the steps, gutter (that can be held on to whilst in the pool), floats and other forms of support.

- The young person may not enjoy the feel/pressure of water, place feet in first and allow time to learn and familiarise themselves with the new sensation.

- The young person may not enjoy the noise of water and the acoustics that surround them.

- The young person may not like being splashed; allow them to remain separate from the group until they become more familiar with the movement of water. Consider using mask/goggles.

- If anxiety turns to distress, consider changing the subject and distract with a different equipment or activity.

- Allow the teaching assistant to be in the water with the young person. Always be on hand to prevent sudden submersion of the face.

- Explain what is going on around them. If their sight/movement is limited, describe what others are doing so they can see/feel reassured that they are doing something similar.

- Depending on the ability of the young person, discuss what they are interested in learning as their lesson may take on a different format to the rest of the class, e.g.

  o Can swimming be used as a relaxation aid for a young person?

  o Do they have to learn a specific stroke? Some young people with developmental coordination difficulties may find breaststroke – an easier stroke to start with.

  o Should they learn basic life/safety skills in water?

  o Should health, competition, rehabilitation and/or fun be the driver for the lesson?

Travel, coordination and balance

- Floats can be used to hold, push, motivate, or hit as targets. Consider the wide variety to help engage the young person, from basic floats to rafts, to woggles, flotation collars, etc.

- When in the water hold on to the side of the pool for extra support. Ask the young person to stand on two feet on the floor and progress to one foot. Holding the side less and less depending on disability and confidence.

Photo 6.5 To float and feel being in the water may sometimes be relaxing for young people

Photo 6.6 Different supportive floats can be fun and purposeful to aid flotation

■ Practise controlled submission of head. Recovery and balance as they resurface.

■ Ask the young person to travel away from the side, a short distance in and back – walking small steps and larger steps, jumping, hopping and lunging. Increase the distance.

■ Introduce arm movements; lift up, out, by side, up and down, in front and behind head.

Buoyancy

Consider these activities in a warm temperature pool.

■ This is a good opportunity for those young people with movement disabilities to feel weightless and control their own movements in the water. Therefore, ask the young person whether they need or would like to use equipment to assist with their buoyancy within the water.

■ Allow the young person to use a woggle under the arms/legs and perform on the front or back or both.

Streamlining

■ Can the young person use different body parts to push away from the wall/jump off the floor into the streamline position? Use another young person to demonstrate the position if need be.

■ Can the young person stand on the floor and perform the streamline position by standing vertical in shallow water?

■ Can the young person put markers down on the floor for peer/self to aim for?

■ Start with back streamlining to avoid water going into face (if this is an issue).

Rotation and orientation

■ Consider standing rotation first to increase confidence.

■ Can the young person rotate from front to back or back to front? Consider using wall/lane ropes to aid momentum in rotating.

■ If appropriate, the young person could perform star floats, mushroom floats, hand stands into rolls and forward/backwards rolls.

■ The young person could also instruct peers on key points on the performance of skills.

Sculling

■ Ask the young person whether they would like to travel on their front/back. The back scull will be easier for most young people first.

■ Set short distance to begin with. Use assistance aids if necessary.

■ Use another young person to assist in demonstrating the movement.

■ Manually help rotate hands and feet to support the young person to follow the movement pattern. Ask the young person if they are happy for you to do this first before moving them automatically.

■ Pull buoys can be used to support their legs (if applicable), and a woggle can be placed behind their back (if applicable).

■ The young person can observe peers and also instruct key points on how to perform the skill correctly and could use peer assessment cards for this.

Aquatic breathing

- Rehearse putting face in water from a standing position (if necessary).

- Encourage the blowing movement to enhance exhalation.

- Allow the young person to practise explosive breathing (blowing air out in larger amounts) or trickle breathing (blowing air out in smaller but more consistent amounts).

- Practise sideways rotation of the head; ask which side the young person prefers.

- Be close to the wall and discuss which breathing technique they wish to try front/side, etc.

- Use visual instruction cards to allow for the development of learning and understanding.

Exiting the pool

- Include the young person in a discussion on how best to exit the pool.

- Encourage the young person to exit on their own as much as possible and only when the teacher is ready. Ensure that there is plenty of space, and make sure the young person observes safety and patience in waiting for their turn.

- If physically able, the young person can pull themselves out of the pool and complete the exercise by remaining sitting on the poolside.

- Encourage verbal instructions throughout the process. Focus on safety.

- Can the young person demonstrate/instruct others within a peer group, by using an observation sheet to build knowledge of safety?

Photo 6.7 Allow the young person to practise safely exiting the pool

The strokes

Swimming for young people who may have difficulty seeing, even when wearing glasses

Key considerations

This list is in no particular order, nor is it essential to complete each and every time. It provides suggestions of *some* of the ways in which you can support the young person in your class. Some may be more relevant than others, so select what may work best for you. Safety and safe practice are paramount throughout, and only you know what is appropriate for the young people in your Physical Education (PE) lessons.

Before the lesson

■ Where possible, give an indication of what you will be doing before the actual lesson. This can be given in advance, potentially 24 hours, especially if the young person is anxious.

■ Ask the young person to contribute to your ideas of inclusion. Empower them.

■ Ask the young person if they wish to work with a friend/group for particular activities. Consider doing this discreetly at first if you do not know the young person.

■ Ask the young person if they wish for you to share some do's and don'ts to the class about visual awareness. The young person may wish to lead this themselves but allow them the choice. Create an atmosphere where the class feel comfortable to ask questions about visual awareness in a positive, considerate way.

■ Use brightly coloured equipment to assist with direction and highlighting obstacles. Planning of such equipment should be thought of ahead of the lesson.

■ Allow the young person to have a safe word that can be used by all to protect each other, so the young person can orientate where people are around them. A common word is 'voy', meaning I am close and know you are there but proceed with caution; the word is intended to be repeated over and over to give perspective of where the person is.

■ Allow the young person to orientate themselves around the area.

■ Encourage peers to work in consideration of the young person who may have additional needs, especially if they can see the young person may be in danger. Specific instructions could be given to one peer to help clarify information given by the teacher to the young person.

■ It is valuable to allow all young people to experience working with others outside of their friendship group.

(Continued)

During the lesson

■ Try to indicate the direction of movement by placing brightly coloured items for the young person to identify.

■ Encourage peers to 'look out' for the young person if they see them in danger.

■ Observe if the young person is challenged enough. Observe if they appear to be isolated and decide how you may wish to address this.

■ If there is a teaching assistant assigned to the young person, consider asking for an update of the progress.

After the lesson

■ Allow the young person to provide feedback on what worked well for them.

■ Seek out if the young person felt challenged enough.

■ Personally reflect on the suitability of your lesson.

OPEN – everyone can be included with very little modification

■ Ask the young person if they require a guide to walk along the poolside or into the pool.
■ Could use a tether if the young person does not wish to hold hands along the poolside.
■ Section off an area in the pool and explain to the group that this is a safe channel/area for the young person.
■ Allow the young people to be close to the wall and to begin in the shallow depth of the pool.
■ If appropriate, provide the young person with a session plan prior to the lesson so they can familiarise themselves with the tasks set out.

MODIFIED – Using changes to Space, Task, Equipment, People (STEP) to include all

■ Progressions of the strokes should remain largely the same.
■ Young people can see/feel demonstrations, and the teacher can show different versions of the activity to all the young people. Go through various degrees of difficulty so the young person has a selection of entry points into the activity.
■ Teacher can explain the key points of the arms/legs of front crawl. Start with legs if possible, using two floats, and then progress to the arms when ready/breathing, etc. Allow the young person to place hands on top of the teacher's arm whilst demonstrating to feel the movement.
■ Floats can be introduced to stimulate learning and support activities.
■ Allow a teaching assistant to be present in the water if necessary.
■ When swimming, encourage the young person to use stroke counts for determining the distance of the pool.
■ Tappers can be used (broom handle) to alert the young person they are close to the wall. The teacher should reach over into the water using the tapper to tap the young person gently.
■ Working with a peer throughout the lesson can build confidence and provide leadership opportunities for others.

PARALLEL – activities delivered simultaneously which allow for different starting points

- Young people can access laminated work sheets with large font, in a variety of colours and images to aid learning and understanding.
- Introduce the use of floats/woggles when learning particular strokes. Cards can be used in isolation or as a teaching aid to break the skill into stages such as two floats, one float, no floats and full stroke stations.

SPECIFIC – purposeful related activity to develop or enhance a skill

- Assistance aids may be needed more here if the young person is anxious.
- The teaching assistant (if possible) can assist in one-to-one skill development.
- The teacher can question the young person to ensure that there is clear understanding.

DISABILITY – introducing disability-specific sports

- View and promote links to https://britishblindsport.org.uk/. The young person can join mainstream clubs if coaches are blind aware.

Reverse integration

- Ask the class to travel with their eyes closed whilst walking swimming. See how well they maintain a straight line.
- Use a tapper to assist the whole class if swimming close to the wall.

Swimming for young people who may have hearing difficulty, even when using a hearing aid. This can also incorporate linguistic difficulties

Key considerations

This list is in no particular order, nor is it essential to complete each and every time. It provides suggestions of *some* of the ways in which you can support the young person in your class. Some may be more relevant than others, so select what may work best for you. Safety and safe practice are paramount throughout, and only you know what is appropriate for the young people in your PE lessons.

Before the lesson

- Where possible, give an indication of what you will be doing before the actual lesson. This can be given in advance, potentially 24 hours, especially if the young person is anxious.
- Ask the young person to contribute to your ideas of inclusion. Empower them.

- Ask the young person if they wish to work with a friend/group for particular activities. Consider doing this discreetly at first if you do not know the young person.

- Ask the young person if they wish for you to share some do's and don'ts to the class about D/deaf awareness. The young person may wish to lead this themselves but allow them the choice. Create an atmosphere where the class feel comfortable to ask questions about D/deaf awareness in a positive, considerate way.

- Consider teaching some basic signs that the whole class can use.

- Not every deaf person knows sign language, not every deaf person can read lips and not every deaf person is able to speak.

- Encourage peers to work in consideration of the young person who may have additional needs, especially if they can see the young person may be in danger. Specific instructions could be given to one peer to help clarify information given by the teacher to the young person.

- It is valuable to allow all young people to experience working with others outside of their friendship group.

- Make sure you decide on an emergency evacuation of the pool system before the young person enters the water, and practise it!

- Remove hearing devices and place somewhere where the young person can access them if they need them. Hearing aids do not like moisture, and the heat in swimming pools could affect the working of the device.

- For advice on cochlear implants, refer to the parents/Special Educational Needs Coordinator/Education Health Care Plan.

During the lesson

- Use facial expression and hand/body gestures to assist with learning.
- Demonstrate *everything*!
- If using lines (follow the leader type activities), allow the young person to be second in the queue so they can follow their peer.
- Use visual commands (hand up to halt play instead of a whistle).
- Ensure classmates are aware of changes/adaptations and ask them to cooperate when activity is stopped or to help reiterate instructions to the young person.

After the lesson

- Allow the young person to provide feedback on what worked well for them.
- Seek out if the young person felt challenged enough.
- Personally reflect on the suitability of your lesson.

OPEN – everyone can be included with very little modification

■ If the young person wears a hearing device, this will need to be removed before they enter the water. The young person needs to be aware this will happen and may need reassurance from teachers and peers. It is possible to allow them access to the aids should they need but must come out of the water and be placed in the ear with dry hands.
■ Peers need to be made aware that the young person may have no/little hearing at all compared to when they wear a hearing device.
■ Provide a brief lesson/key points of whichever stroke you are teaching before the lesson. Laminate the lesson plan so this can be referred to throughout.
■ Ask the young person if they want a peer to work with and follow throughout the lesson.
■ Make sure pupils/teacher is facing the young person who has a hearing impairment (if the young person reads lips) or use sign language and signals throughout the lessons.
■ Make sure the class are aware of how to attract the attention of the young person with a hearing impairment. Agree on a hand gesture and allow all to practise this safety drill on a regular basis.
■ The teacher can demonstrate the skills on the side of the pool, and use peers to perform to the class and the young person in the pool.

MODIFIED – Using changes to Space, Task, Equipment, People (STEP) to include all

■ Organise in smaller groups and ensure that the young person is working with someone they feel comfortable with.
■ Allow the young person to use floats (if necessary) to assist with balance and confidence.
■ May have to break down progressions more if the concept is not grasped.
■ The teacher can ask the young person open-ended questions to allow them to introduce their own ideas to the skills.
■ Make sure explanations of the activities are shown to the young person; the teacher could select a good demonstrator and discuss with the young person/class why this pupil has been selected.

PARALLEL – activities delivered simultaneously which allow for different starting points

■ Swimming progressions may remain the same, but if parallel tasks are required, introduce different stations of activity to break the technique down, using floats, isolating body parts, practising streamlining/ buoyancy, etc.

SPECIFIC – purposeful related activity to develop or enhance a skill

■ Assistance aids maybe needed more here if the young person is anxious.
■ The teaching assistant (if possible) can assist in one-to-one skill development.
■ The teacher can question the young person to ensure that there is clear understanding.

DISABILITY – introducing disability-specific sports

■ A pathway to elite deaf swimming does exist via https://ukdeafsport.org.uk/.

Reverse integration
■ Allow children to wear goggles and communicate beneath the water. Allow them to learn and share signs.

Photo 6.8 Using the side of the pool can aid with skill development

Swimming for young people that may have difficulty remembering or concentrating

Key considerations

This list is in no particular order, nor is it essential to complete each and every time. It provides suggestions of *some* of the ways in which you can support the young person in your class. Some may be more relevant than others, so select what may work best for you. Safety and safe practice are paramount throughout, and only you know what is appropriate for the young people in your PE lessons.

Before the lesson

- Where possible give an indication of what you will be doing before the actual lesson. This can be given in advance, potentially 24 hours before, especially if the young person is anxious.

- Ask the young person to contribute to your ideas of inclusion. Empower them.

- Ask the young person if they wish to work with a friend/group for particular activities. Consider doing this discreetly at first if you do not know the young person.

- Ask the young person if they wish for you to share some do's and don'ts to the class about processing information. The young person may wish to lead this themselves but allow them the choice. Create an atmosphere where the class feel comfortable to ask questions about other's particular learning and processing requirements in a positive, considerate way.

- Consider having PECS to assist with equipment and order of activities ahead and throughout the session if appropriate. Microsoft Immersive Reader is useful to turn words into pictures.

- Encourage peers to work in consideration of the young person who may have additional needs, especially if they can see the young person may be in danger. Specific instructions could be given to one peer to help clarify information given by the teacher to the young person.

- It is valuable to allow all young people to experience working with others outside of their friendship group.

- Allow more time to change into and out of swimming kit.

- Some young people may not enjoy the sensation of the pressure of water around them, consider a backup plan/activity should the young person have to be taken out of the pool due to distress.

During the lesson

- Have signs and colours on the wall to help use as reference points for directional sense.

- Always point out and reinforce the direction they are travelling to and when.

- Provide a list of activities that will be experiencing and ask the young person to tick them off as they proceed through the lesson.

- Provide a glossary of terms to help with new terminology.

- Reference TV characters (as suggested in Appendix A) that may support the young person in visualising and copying particular actions.

- Encourage the young person to ask for clarity if necessary.

- Allow rest breaks if the young person seems anxious.

- Provide a checklist of targets for the young person to work through and tick off as they go.

- Be ready to repeat your instructions but avoid re-phrasing, and try to keep your language the same.

After the lesson

- Allow the young person to provide feedback on what worked well for them.

- Seek out if the young person felt challenged enough, did their cognition or processing improve?

- Personally reflect on the suitability of your lesson.

(Continued)

OPEN – everyone can be included with very little modification

- Lesson plans/resource cards can be sent to the teaching assistant/young person prior to the session. Use diagrams/photos if necessary.
- The teacher can use the same warm-up/activity each week so that it is familiar; this will allow the young person to become comfortable from the start of the lesson.
- Ask if the young person needs a helper throughout the lesson.
- Pair the young person with a peer who they feel confident to work with.
- Ensure that there are separate areas for the young person to swim/perform the skills instructed if needed.
- It would be advised to inform the class why some students may be separate to the main lesson.
- Allow the young person to stand up when needed.

MODIFIED – Using changes to Space, Task, Equipment, People (STEP) to include all

- Explanations may take longer to be processed, so allow more time for activity (if required).
- Instructions may need to be repeated to ensure understanding and try to use the same terms.
- The teacher can encourage the young person to answer questions to check their understanding of the task set.
- The young person can decide what type of equipment they wish to use during performing and progressing stroke elements.
- Change equipment/distance to suit and move closer/further apart to create/reduce challenge.

PARALLEL – activities delivered simultaneously which allow for different starting points

- As above but the young person may need an assistant with them or a responsible peer.

SPECIFIC – purposeful related activity to develop or enhance a skill

- As above.

DISABILITY – introducing disability-specific sports

- There are organisations that can help raise awareness for all young people. There could be an opportunity for you to promote mainstream sport as well as impairment-specific competitive pathways such as the Special Olympics. Try:

https://www.mencap.org.uk/about-us/what-we-do/mencap-sport
http://www.uksportsassociation.org/
https://www.specialolympics.org/

Swimming for young people who may have difficulty walking or climbing stairs

Key considerations

This list is in no particular order, nor is it essential to complete each and every time. It provides suggestions of some of the ways in which you can support the young person in your class. Some may be more relevant than others, so select what may work best for you. Safety and safe practice are paramount throughout, and only you know what is appropriate for the young people in your PE lessons.

Before the lesson

■ Where possible, give an indication of what you will be doing before the actual lesson. This can be given in advance, potentially 24 hours, especially if the young person is anxious.

■ Ask the young person to contribute to your ideas of inclusion. Empower them.

■ Ask the young person if they wish to work with a friend/group for particular activities. Consider doing this discreetly at first if you do not know the young person.

■ Ask the young person if they wish for you to share some do's and don'ts to the class about wheelchair etiquette/walker (if using one). The young person may wish to lead this themselves but allow them the choice. Create an atmosphere where the class feel comfortable to ask questions about wheelchair, walker or movement in a positive, considerate way.

■ Encourage peers to work in consideration of the young person who may have additional needs, especially if they can see the young person may be in danger. Specific instructions could be given to one peer to help clarify information given by the teacher to the young person.

■ It is valuable to allow all young people to experience working with others outside of their friendship group.

During the lesson

■ Be realistic with the amount of the activity the young person is required to do.

■ Allow support aids, bolsters or standing platforms and use of foam gym wedges to support movement. Also allow partners for support.

■ Encourage the young person to ask for clarity if necessary.

■ Allow rest breaks if the young person seems anxious.

(Continued)

After the lesson

■ Allow the young person to provide feedback on what worked well for them.

■ Seek out if the young person felt challenged enough.

■ Personally reflect on the suitability of your lesson.

OPEN – everyone can be included with very little modification

■ Ensure that all movements are broken down appropriately.
■ Ensure that all technical points are discussed before progressing to the next task.
■ The teacher will also need to be aware that some skills may need to be revisited throughout the lesson.
■ Ensure the same warm-up is introduced each week so the young person can start the lesson as soon as possible to aid understanding and to calm potential stress levels, etc.
■ Ensure that the young person can either hold on to the wall or sit on the steps as extra support when hearing the instructions of the skills/strokes/lesson.

MODIFIED – Using changes to Space, Task, Equipment, People (STEP) to include all

■ Discuss and agree on the aims of the lesson. Is the focus on stroke development or rehabilitation/ recovery/water safety? This may then focus the lesson for a more student-centred approach (see SPECIFIC section below, as stroke development may be inappropriate for the young person.
■ Ensure that they have enough space to enter the water with/without the assistant as support (where appropriate).
■ Ensure that the young person works with other peers within the lesson.
■ Give the young person shorter tasks and limited information such as two/three key points before performing the skill.
■ Suitable floats can be selected by the young person to assist in activities.
■ Allow frequent rest breaks if necessary.

PARALLEL – activities delivered simultaneously which allow for different starting points

■ Depending on the ability, set specific workstations that may develop particular skills or functions for the young person. The young person can help design/select these activities.
■ One station could be part body submersion, whole body, or head. Another could be floating with assistance, for example, using a float or support from a teaching assistant, encourage propulsion on back, etc.
■ Allow the young person to work with peers/teaching assistant depending on the additional needs of the young person.

SPECIFIC – purposeful related activity to develop or enhance a skill

■ If the young person is unable to enter the water, use observation sheets/peer assessment sheets throughout the lesson to help support teaching points, for example, creative tasks such as designing a synchronized routine for peers to execute. Encourage the cognitive and affective learning domains.

- Refer to a key skills/strokes card throughout the lesson to reinforce key points.
- If the young person can get into the water, then practise using equipment to isolate the skill of either legs or arms to build understanding and potentially strength.
- Refer to their Education Health Care Plan in order to assist with rehabilitation/recovery.
- For young people with cerebral palsy, being in the water can provide valuable movement skills as body parts are supported by water and floats.

DISABILITY – introducing disability-specific sports

- Raise awareness of national governing bodies (WheelPower, Cerebral Palsy, Dwarf Sports, etc.) and consider local or regional development groups.
- The website https://www.wheelpower.org.uk/ includes powerchair activities.
- The website http://www.cpsport.org/ includes framed activities.
- https://www.dsauk.org/
- http://limbpower.com/
- Also look at mainstream national governing bodies as some do have disability strands.

Swimming for young people who may have difficulty with upper body movement and control

Key considerations

This list is in no particular order, nor is it essential to complete each and every time. It provides suggestions of *some* of the ways in which you can support the young person in your class. Some may be more relevant than others, so select what may work best for you. Safety and safe practice are paramount throughout, and only you know what is appropriate for the young people in your PE lessons.

Before the lesson

- Where possible, give an indication of what you will be doing before the actual lesson. This can be given in advance, potentially 24 hours, especially if the young person is anxious.

- Ask the young person to contribute to your ideas of inclusion. Empower them.

- Ask the young person if they wish to work with a friend/group for particular activities. Consider doing this discreetly at first if you do not know the young person.

- Ask the young person if they wish for you to share some do's and don'ts to the class about limb movement. The young person may wish to lead this themselves but allow them the choice. Create an atmosphere where the class feel comfortable to ask questions about disability awareness in a positive, considerate way.

(Continued)

- Encourage peers to work in consideration of the young person who may have additional needs, especially if they can see the young person may be in danger. Specific instructions could be given to one peer to help clarify information given by the teacher to the young person.

- It is valuable to allow all young people to experience working with others outside of their friendship group.

During the lesson

- Be mindful of balance.

- Check in with the young person on their engagement/preference.

- Encourage the young person to ask for clarity if necessary.

- Allow rest breaks if the young person seems anxious.

- Make sure the young person is being challenged in the activity you have set.

After the lesson

- Allow the young person to provide feedback on what worked well for them.

- Seek out if the young person felt challenged enough, did their skills improve?

- Personally reflect on the suitability of your lesson.

OPEN – everyone can be included with very little modification

- Young people can be shown diagrams and visual aids for the lessons on how they will be included.
- Reassure the young person that progressions will go at their pace.
- A variety of distances can be travelled/swum throughout the lesson.
- Can use fins if appropriate to help the young person move through the water more easily.

MODIFIED – Using changes to Space, Task, Equipment, People (STEP) to include all

- The young person can be given enough space and support within the water.
- Consider having blocks in the water so the young person can stand and rest.
- Modify swimming distances.
- Start with activities on their back.
- Develop aquatic breathing or allow the use of snorkel.
- The young person can decide what type of equipment they wish to use and when to progress to performing elements of the stroke.

PARALLEL – activities delivered simultaneously which allow for different starting points

- Consider examples above as the young person can help select how they wish to be engaged so the activity becomes purposeful to their quality of living.

SPECIFIC – purposeful related activity to develop or enhance a skill

- Assistance aids may be needed more here if the young person is anxious.
- The teaching assistant (if possible) can assist in one-to-one skill development.
- Use demonstrations/peer observation.
- The young person can use woggles/noodles under the arms/stomach to support the body and allow the young person to use their legs in a kicking action – alternating or simulation leg action.

DISABILITY – introducing disability-specific sports

Consider showing the group how Paralympians/individuals who may be amputees or no upper body limbs swim (http://limbpower.com/).

Diving

For key considerations for each section below, please refer to the 'The Strokes' section.

Diving for young people who may have difficulty seeing, even when wearing glasses

OPEN – everyone can be included with very little modification

- Ask the young person if they require a guide.
- The guide can be in or out of the water.
- Ensure the young person feels comfortable with the task and is clear with the depth of water.
- Allow a peer to work with the young person.

MODIFIED – Using changes to Space, Task, Equipment, People (STEP) to include all

- The young person can start in the progressive stages and participate without STEP depending on the ability and confidence of the young person.
- Orientation and confidence building activities may have to be the task adaption.
- Discuss with the young person if diving is a skill they wish to develop rather than improving stroke development or life-saving skills. Amend the task to suit this or look at separate activities.
- The young person can demonstrate different jumps into the water if a dive is becoming difficult.

PARALLEL – activities delivered simultaneously which allow for different starting points

- The young person can use worksheet to build understanding and provide large, bright targets on the pool floor to help aim for a particular space. Audio queues could also be used to increase directional awareness.
- Parallel activities can remain the same for the group but having different stages of dive, e.g. seated, crouch, etc.

(Continued)

SPECIFIC – purposeful related activity to develop or enhance a skill

- If the school owns trampolines/harness, the start of the forward movement can be rehearsed prior to introducing water.
- If the teaching assistant is in the water with the young person, it may assist in confidence and quality of movement. Progressions are as follows:
  o 1. Push and glide
  o 2. Surface dive into deeper water (practice in shallow water first)
  o 3. Sitting dive
  o 4. Kneeling dive
  o 5. Standing dive
  o 6. Off block (if appropriate)

DISABILITY – introducing disability-specific sports

- View and promote links to https://britishblindsport.org.uk/. The young person can join mainstream clubs if coaches are blind aware.

Reverse integration
- The young person can verbally signal 'go'/dive' for other peers.
- Give numbers to the group so that only selected numbers dive at any one time and the young person can lead this.

Diving for young people that may have hearing difficulty, even when using a hearing aid. This can also incorporate linguistic difficulties

OPEN – everyone can be included with very little modification

- Explain the key points as much as you can prior to the removal of any hearing devices. Use laminated worksheet to support the lesson. If the plan could be given in advance, this may reassure the young person more.
- Make sure that the young person can clearly see and understand the lips (if they can lip read).
- Develop hand gestures to support understanding and safety.

MODIFIED – Using changes to Space, Task, Equipment, People (STEP) to include all

- The young person can start in the progressive stages and participate without STEP depending on the ability and confidence of the young person.
- The young person can demonstrate different jumps into the water if a dive is becoming difficult.

PARALLEL – activities delivered simultaneously which allow for different starting points

- No real adaptions are needed here unless particular stages of the dive need to be improved (see above).

■ Encourage the use of assistance aids, make sure the progressions for diving safely are adhered to.
■ The young person can instruct a small group of pupils on the key points from the worksheet.
■ Progressions from the section above could also be used.
■ The young person can use relevant self-assessment sheets to aid personal improvement.

■ If the mainstream club is Deaf aware, full integration should be possible.

Reverse integration
■ The young person can verbally signal 'go'/dive' for other peers.
■ Give numbers to the group so that only selected numbers dive at any one time and the young person can lead this. See the 'strokes section' for children who may have trouble hearing for deaf opportunities.

Diving for young people that may have difficulty remembering or concentrating

■ The young person can become familiar with the deep water by just looking down at the depth before undertaking any diving practice. Can also be done via push and glide.
■ Ensure that the skill is broken down and key points are focussed on throughout.
  o Hands together
  o Head between hands
  o Push away from the wall to ensure safety
  o The teacher can repeat these key points of safety throughout the whole lesson to the young person and the rest of the class.
  o Stage-by-stage pictures may help the young person understand the concept.

■ The teacher can use verbal/non-verbal communication throughout the diving practice concentrating on safety for all.
■ The teacher can use effective demonstrations throughout.
■ The young person can start in the progressive stages and participate without STEP depending on the ability and confidence of the young person.
■ The young person can demonstrate different jumps into the water if a dive is becoming difficult.
■ Could practise diving from the surface to retrieve objects from the bottom of the pool.

(Continued)

Photo 6.9 Retrieving objects beneath the water can provide an exciting challenge for some young people

PARALLEL – activities delivered simultaneously which allow for different starting points

■ As above.

SPECIFIC – purposeful related activity to develop or enhance a skill

■ The teacher can allow all pupils to see a good demonstration of each stage of diving and to discuss with class the key points by using the instruction card.
■ Allow the young person to work alongside a teaching assistant or peer to develop the stages as and when confidence and comprehension of the skills are displayed.

DISABILITY – introducing disability-specific sports

Please refer to 'the strokes' section for those who have 'difficulty in remembering' … for more detail.

■ The young person can oversee the feedback station and observation of pairs.

Diving for young people who may have difficulty walking or climbing stairs

OPEN – everyone can be included with very little modification

■ Inform the young person using a manual wheelchair that when coming into the pool area, their wheelchair will not be used within the pool, but an additional chair may be used on the poolside.
■ The w/c or walker will be moved to where the young person needs it when exiting the pool. Additional towels may be required to protect the w/c.
■ The young person can use the side of the pool/blocks to sit/stand/kneel as appropriate.
■ Ensure that diving skills are broken down and each stage is practised several times before progressing.
■ Teachers can revisit different stages for the young person and others within the class.
■ Be mindful that the young person may get cold quicker.

MODIFIED – Using changes to Space, Task, Equipment, People (STEP) to include all

- The young person can sit on the side of the pool/block to progress the diving skill.
- Shorter swimming distances after the dive may be necessary.
- The young person can ensure that the stronger leg/foot is able to provide support on the poolside to prevent slipping.
- Ensure that the young person works with other peers within the lesson.
- Give the young person shorter tasks and limited information such as two or three key points before performing the skill.

PARALLEL – activities delivered simultaneously which allow for different starting points

- As above.
- Use instruction cards/ self/peer assessment.
- Pair pupils together of equal or closely matched ability to allow for observation and feedback throughout the lesson.
- The young person can have enough space to practise the skill to increase confidence and ensure that they show their skill progression to the teacher/peers.

SPECIFIC – purposeful related activity to develop or enhance a skill

- As above.
- The young person is also able to practise off a smaller height block to enter the pool at a lower height.
- The young person can practise leaning forward into the dive from a smaller height before progressing higher.
- The young person can aim for a point in front of them away from the walls to ensure that the dive is being performed safely.
- Practise using a range of the stages to ensure confidence throughout.

DISABILITY – introducing disability-specific sports

- See 'the strokes' section for those who may have difficulty in walking or climbing.
- If someone is assisting the young person whilst diving, make sure the assistant stands to the side of the young person.
- Assistance aid may need to hold the arm/hand of the young person to help with balance – or another object can be used if appropriate.

Photo 6.10 Modify the entry to the water that suits the confidence level of the young person

Diving for young people who may have difficulty with upper body movement and control

OPEN – everyone can be included with very little modification

■ The young person can use the side of the pool/blocks to sit or stand on (if appropriate).

MODIFIED – Using changes to Space, Task, Equipment, People (STEP) to include all

■ The young person can ensure that the stronger hand/arm is underneath the weaker hand, 'performing a streamline position'. Ensure that the head is protected throughout the dive.
■ The young person can demonstrate different jumps into the water if a dive is becoming difficult.

PARALLEL – activities delivered simultaneously which allow for different starting points

■ As above.

SPECIFIC – purposeful related activity to develop or enhance a skill

■ The young person can practise having their arms down by their side as an option; however, ensure that the young person uses a lower height block to begin with.

DISABILITY – introducing disability-specific sports

■ http://limbpower.com/

Additional resources

Appendix A

Using TV/movie characters to help assist with the young person's understanding of physical movements

This concept can be used to help young people with processing impairments to understand large movements in a game scenario. Not all young people know what we mean when we say 'attack', 'defend' or 'stand with tension'. If you know what characters they watch on TV or in films you can try and use those characters as points of reference. Make sure the individual or group is aware of the character that you want to use (have a few backups, just in case). Discuss briefly how the character may move/behave, allowing young people to copy these movements if they choose to (depending on age). Developing these characterisations into actual team play may take practice, so it could be used in a parallel or separate section of your lesson. It will also be useful to use a variety of different characters, depending on age, interest and motivation.

For example, show a picture of Shrek and discuss his character, then ask questions such as 'How might Shrek stop donkey leaving the room?' and 'What would he do with his hands and his legs?', and then liken this to the skill you want them to develop. The young people can respond with words or actions in relation to a defensive stance in basketball.

Appendix B

What is a visual trail?

A sequence of simple drawings that a group follows around a set designated area.

Instructions

Give the pupils a certain time to create their visual trail. As a group they must create mini maps by drawing key points on numerous pieces of paper provided.

The group selects a key aspect within the landscape that they wish to 'send' the following group to. Someone within the group draws the key features on paper to resemble the features, and it should be a quick, simple diagram. The whole group then moves to the aspect they have drawn and then select a new visual clue from the landscape to draw the clue onto a new piece of paper. This continues, and the landscape features should be easy to recognise. Agree the start and finish points of the trail.

Tip: When the group who is creating the visual trail and when they get to their designated clue, turn 360° to look for a different direction to travel in rather than just forwards; this should provide more challenge for the following group.

This activity will be suitable for all young people to do together. Some groups will create large, complex maps that cover distances, and others can create simple and smaller versions too.

Appendix C

Additional resources for games – homemade or low-cost versions

This section may help with some equipment:

- For balls that may need bells in them (audio), place the desired ball in a plastic bag, and tie up the bag and use.

- Sometimes deflating the balls allows for more control if movement is limited.

- Create your own simulation spectacles by buying industrial safety goggles and either paint or cover aspects of the glasses.

- Use a drainpipe to help as a boccia ramp.

- A narrow piece of plastic sheeting can assist for new age kurling.

- Use scrunched up newspaper (surrounded by masking tape) to create boccia balls.

- Use a bed sheet as a parachute. Cut holes in the parachute to create a different, target game.

- Use dog throwing sticks to help pick up tennis balls.

- Dog toys on strings are very good to fling.

- Use a washing line to allow young people to run blindfolded. Have two people at each end keeping the line taut, while the person in the middle goes from A to B, blindfolded. Safety measures can be put in place by attaching an empty pen case as a handle to hold (to avoid friction).

Resource card A: Colour ball

A modified game of netball that develops movement together as an attacking team

What you need

■ Any suitable flat and clean indoor playing area

■ Designated areas denoted by markers that show the point zones

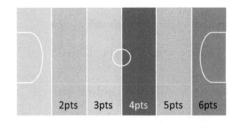

The aim

■ The attacking team have ten passes to see how far they can move down the court to score. The opposing time will attempt to intercept.

How you play

■ You cannot move if you have the ball.

■ You can hold the ball up to five seconds.

■ Marking can be 1.5 m away from people with and without the ball.

■ Only attacking team can score in the coloured area.

■ Play starts from the back line of the lowest scoring area (yellow).

■ Direction of play is only one way.

■ Teams alternate after each attempt.

How to modify the space

■ Use half court or a third of the netball court for smaller sided teams.

■ Give specific areas to students to work in to prevent all moving to the same space; this would prevent overcrowding.

■ To challenge pupils, remove colours so that there are less areas to score in.

■ Use a sensory dot ball, swirl ball or lightweight ball in skill practices to develop students' passing and receiving 1 v 1.

How to modify the task

■ Use a sensory dot ball, swirl ball or lightweight ball in skill practices to develop students passing and receiving 1 v 1.

■ Change the number of passes or if the defenders intercept the ball, the teams swap over at that point rather than after a certain number of passes.

- Point system may also be changed to higher numbers further down to encourage students to want to get to those areas.

- You could score into a hoop rather than a net.

- Coloured areas could be taken away and nets provided for additional practice.

- Game came be played in both directions.

How to modify the equipment

- A range of balls could be utilised in the full game: lightweight handball, volleyball, sensory dot ball, "Oball", tactile flashing bumpy ball and sponge ball (if played indoors).

How to modify people groupings

- Reduce the size of teams from 7 v 7 to 5 v 5 or apply overload to teams so that the teams are unequal. Remove the defenders.

Key considerations

- This game is suitable for students with learning difficulties, cognitive development difficulties, wheelchair users, delayed physical development, social learning difficulties, mental health or behavioural issues.

- This game encourages the skills and rules of netball such as passing, defending, moving to scoring end, creating space and team work.

- The areas of court are broken down into coloured sections (use poly spots), and students move into specific coloured zones to score points. The direction of play is in one direction.

Resource card B: Adapted walking netball

A modified game of netball that develops spatial awareness, team spirit and basic sending and receiving skills

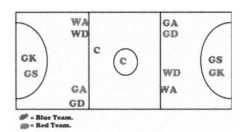

- = Blue Team.
- = Red Team.

What you need
■ Any suitable flat and clean indoor playing area
■ A variety of balls to select from
■ Markers to help display designated areas of play

The aim

■ To play a modified version of the game at walking pace.

How you play
■ Everyone must walk and have one foot in contact with the ground at all times.
■ During play an extra step is allowed if the player has received the ball.
■ Players with the ball are allowed to hold the ball for up to five seconds.
■ Not every position has to be filled.

How to modify the space

■ Play in half court or in end ball style game in one third (positions omitted in this game).

■ Zone a section to include a player who is in a wheelchair.

How to modify the task

■ Practise rules of footwork in small-sided games and in skill practices.

■ Allow longer time on the ball.

How to modify people groupings

■ Reduce the size of teams from 7 v 7 to 5 v 5 and remove wing positions or apply overload to teams so that the teams are unequal.

■ Allow someone to receive the ball for a player who may have low motor ability.

How to modify the equipment

■ Lower nets and varying sizes of netball could be used.

■ Different targets can be used to score; use of gates for players to travel through can be an additional point.

Key considerations

This game is suitable for students with learning difficulties, students with physical development issues, all ability groups, students with low confidence and low self-esteem, students with mental health issues and behavioural issues, students with asthma and other respiratory conditions, students who are over-weight and those returning to sport from injury.

The game is played using all netball positions. The game is played on a full-size netball court with netball and regulation height posts. It is a great way for students to learn the game of netball at a slower pace and can apply the skills. It can ensure students are all involved in netball and allows for a variety of abilities to play together.

Resource card C: Buddy netball

A modified game of netball that develops collaborative team play between players

What you need

- Any suitable flat and clean indoor playing area

- A variety of balls to select from

- Markers to help display designated areas of play

The aim

- To play a modified version of netball in pairs. One player remains on court whilst the other observes them off court. The players decide when to swap roles, but must discuss their tactics and progress.

How you play

- You cannot move when you have the ball.

- Three seconds before a pass needs to be made.

- Marking should be 1 m away (with and without the ball).

- Shoot to score as in netball.

How to modify the space

- Play in half court or in end ball style game in one third (positions omitted in this game).

- This game is good for when space is limited as some schools may only have

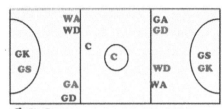

one netball court, and this prevents students from not being active through the change-over buddy scenario.

How to modify the task

"Buddy" pairs can be given time to work on skills together out of a game/competitive scenario, and they can be provided with a specific focus, given tasks to stretch and challenge them, or complete peer-assessment tasks on the sideline or in skills practice.

How to modify the equipment

- Lower nets and varying sizes of netball could be used.

How to modify people

- Students could be given the opportunity to swap positions, which may mean they have a new buddy.

- Teachers may wish to pair up according to ability levels.

Key considerations

This game is suitable for mixed ability classes, students with social interaction difficulties, low confidence and self-esteem and physical disability.

The concept means that students who are struggling to learn the game, are feeling under-confident, are of a low ability, have a physical disability or struggle to maintain activity for sustained periods of time will play netball with regular rules and positions, but each player will have a 'buddy'.

The buddy is usually a player who is more able but can be applied with students of similar ability or purely friendship pairs to give students more confidence and enjoyment and to be more engaged in the game. If swaps have not occurred, the teacher should facilitate the change so that players go on for at least a few minutes before they can swap again.

Teaching assistant cards

Teaching Assistant Card 1 (suggested for athletics/games)

Throwing for young people who may have difficulty walking or climbing stairs

Learning Outcome: To improve accuracy when throwing.

This card is designed to help young people that may have to develop their skills separately from the class with a peer, teaching assistant or within a small group. Always try to involve the young person in decision making regarding what they want to achieve within the lesson. Try to focus on what they can do rather than what they cannot and follow the teacher's teaching points.

Key Considerations

- Practise sending a ball or other throwing equipment to a person or a target.

- Distances can be close or further away to challenge the individual.

- Use a variety of targets (bucket, hoop, line, cone) and start with a range of small, large and light throwing implements.

- Consider using a ramp to propel items, if needed. A drainpipe can be used (if cut in half and made safe).

Activity 1

Throwing to a static target

- Place a target quite close to the young person to instil confidence and success, move backwards.

- Suggest speed of movement of arm towards and on point of release of item.

- Explore sideways, front on and over shoulder throwing position (depending on item that is being thrown).

- Consider using a tee to send/knock things off if movement is restricted.

Activity 2

Throwing to a partner/moving partner

- With a partner start close and place items in each other's hands and gradually move back, encouraging a throw.

- Explore over arm movements (or underarm, push, nudge or flick) to gauge distance.

- Allow practise and find ways to send the item. Challenge with different distances and force of throw.

- When 'range' is consistent consider asking partner to move side to side, back and forth whilst other send the item to them.

Teaching Assistant Card 2 (suggested for athletics/games)

Throwing for young people who may have difficulty walking or climbing stairs

Learning Outcome: To be able to throw for distance

This card is designed to help young people that may have to develop their skills separately from the class with a peer, teachingassistant or within asmall group. Always try to involve the young person in decision making regarding what they want to achieve within the lesson. Try to focus on what they can do rather than what they cannot and follow the teacher's teaching points.

Key Considerations

- To practise different ways of sending an object as far as the young person can.

- If using a chair, consider how the young person sits as they will need to be seated securely.

- You can fashion the chair /frame so that it is close to something immovable so they young person can use as support or to resist against.

- Use a variety of different objects.

Activity 1

- Explore the range of movement that young person has with their arms and core strength.

- Ask the young person to move a light ball around their body, head, arms to observe mobility (if necessary).

- Experiment with throwing, pushing, flinging, projecting and rolling items away from their body. Start with light equipment or the young person's preference. Question which technique they feel more successful with.

Activity 2

- Experiment with changing the angle of the wheelchair/frame to allow more range of movement from arms or body.

- Experiment with overarm and underarm throws. You can also allow the young person to throw from a backwards position over their head as this may allow more range of movement.

- Use lines or marker cons to provide feedback in terms of successful technique.

Teaching Assistant Card 3 (suggested for athletics/games)

Throwing for young people who may have difficulty seeing, even when wearing glasses

Learning Outcome: To improve accuracy when throwing

This card is designed to help young people that may have to develop their skills separately from the class with a peer, teaching assistant or within a small group. Always try to involve the young person in decision making and what they want to achieve within the lesson. Try to focus on what they can do rather than what they cannot and follow the teacher's teaching points.

Key Considerations

- To practise sending different throwing implements to various targets or a partner.

- Distances can be close or further away to challenge the individual.

- Use a variety of targets and start with large, audible throwing implements. If no audible balls are available put ball in a plastic bag and secure it.

- Explore the space you will be using to throw in with the young person.

*Note: the ball will not carry sound if it is airborne, so make sure you start with something soft to throw/catch.

Activity 1

Throwing to a partner/moving partner

- Start toe to toe facing each other and place object in hands, pass back to and fro. Gradually encourage throwing between the pair. Move backwards to increase distanceCommunication is key between the pair, use names to call for attention, ask 'ready?', and 'sending' and 'caught/dropped'.

- To add in movement one partner say 'left one step'. Other person point to where they think they should send the ball, the other confirms and proceed as previous, constantly calling out person's name to aid with direction.

- Make this a bit quicker, left and right, closer, further away etc.

Activity 2

Throwing to a static target

- Walk the young person to where the targets are and help them measure the distance in order to create a mental picture.

- You can use your finger to draw a pitch or area on the back of their hand to give them placement of the target/s.

- Use their forearm to show scale of how close they may/may not be from the target.

- Move targets according to success and to provide further challenge.

Teaching Assistant Card 4 (suggested for athletics/games)

Throwing for young people who may have difficulty seeing, even when wearing glasses

Learning outcome: To improve throwing for distance

This card is designed to help young people that may have to develop their skills separately from the class with a peer, teaching assistant or within a small group. Always try to involve the young person in decision making and what they want to achieve within the lesson. Try to focus on what they can do rather than what they cannot and follow the teacher's teaching points.

Key Considerations

- Practise sending objects as far as the young person can.

- Explore the area with the young person so they are clear with what direction they will be releasing the item in and how much space they have around them.

- Explore and experiment with different techniques needed for different items when throwing for distance.

Activity 1

- Allow a short amount of time for the young person to make sense of the equipment they wish to throw.

- Consider how the young person stands, try a front ways on position then sideways on.

- Allow them to point to where they intend to throw it and you, as their peer/TA, give them the all clear to throw.

- Walk the young person out to where they have thrown the item so they can gauge distance.

Activity 2

- Encourage the young person to consider getting their body weight behind the throw.

- If overarm, use a transference of weight from back foot through to front foot.

- Opposite arm opposite leg if throwing underarm and maybe more front ways on.

- Explore which item goes furthest for the young person.

Teaching Assistant Card 5 (suggested for athletics/games)

Jumping for young people who have difficulty in seeing, even when wearing glasses

Learning Outcome: To develop jumping for distance

This card is designed to help young people that may have to develop their skills separately from the class with a peer, teaching assistant or within a small group. Always try to involve the young person in decision making and what they want to achieve within the lesson. Try to focus on what they can do rather than what they cannot and follow the teacher's teaching points.

Key Considerations

- To improve confidence at jumping forward from a static position then eventually with a short run up.

- Start with investigating the surroundings, textures of floor mats, sand, gym floors, to make sure young person can try to distinguish landing area.

- As the Teaching Assistant, you need to say when it is safe to jump.

- Ensure the young person knows how to land safely before jumping for distance.

Activity 1

- Reinforce all teaching points delivered by the teacher.

- Allow the young person to stand a short distance away. Call out 'voy' and the young person moves towards the noise.

- Use words rather than demonstrations.

- Start with a standing jump, bend legs (squat position), swing arms back as legs bend. Drive arms forwards, keep feet together and land two footed.

- Allow practise time, two feet to two feet, two feet to one foot, one foot to two.

- Explore combination of jumps, hops, strides to develop balance and confidence.

Activity 2

- Progress by walking one step into a hop (land two footed). Two step and hop etc. Explore with same combinations.

- Build up to 3 stride, jog and hop and land two footed. You must make sure that when the run up is increased the young person needs to be landing in sand rather than the hall floor or mat.

- As the run up increases you should stand at the end of the pit and call the young person's name. The young person points to the direction they are going to run up and you must be ready to stop the young personif they deviate from the run up (as they are running).

- The young person must have a set number of strides within the run up to help them count so as when to take off.

Teaching Assistant Card 6 (suggested for athletics)

Jumping for young people who may have difficulty seeing, even when wearing glasses.

Learning Outcome: To develop skills in jumping for height.

This card is designed to help young people that may have to develop their skills separately from the class with a peer, teaching assistant or within a small group. Always try to involve the young person in decision making and what they want to achieve within the lesson. Try to focus on what they can do rather than what they cannot and follow the teacher's teaching points.

Key Considerations

- To improve confidence at jumping for height.

- Start with investigating the surroundings, textures of floor mats, gym floors, uprights, to make sure the young person can try to distinguish landing area and feel of items around them.

- You must always say when it is safe to jump.

Activity 1

- Reinforce teaching points delivered by the teacher.

- Use a line marking then progress to a small SAQ hurdle, then Eveque type hurdle. Encourage the young person to stand by the line/hurdle and lift their closest leg to the hurdle over and then place their foot the other side, the other leg to follow without touching the barrier. Do this slowly to start.

- Practise this until it becomes a continuous, explosive movement, so that both legs may be off the ground at one time creating a scissor kick type action.

Activity 2

- Once confidence is gained, encourage legs to be lifted even higher but still straight legged.

- When the young person is ready, measure out two of their strides sideways to the barrier. Allow the young person to rehearse the walk, then develop into a dynamic stride towards the barrier. The young person should still be approaching sideways onto the barrier. Use audio queue to tell them they are good to jump or not.

- Maintain technique, gradually raise the barrier.

- Increase run up to 3-4-5 strides. When 5 strides is gained and the young person is clearing the barrier easily, move onto the high jump bed.

Teaching Assistant Card 7 (suggested for athletics)

Running for young people who may have difficulty seeing, even when wearing glasses

Learning Outcome: To develop running for speed or running for distance

This card is designed to help young people that may have to develop their skills separately from the class with a peer, teaching assistant or within a small group. Always try to involve the young person in decision making and what they want to achieve within the lesson. Try to focus on what they can do rather than what they cannot and follow the teacher's teaching points.

Key Considerations

- Pair the young person with someone they feel comfortable with.

- Provide a bib (to act as a tether).

- Allow the two to experiment walking using the tether and how they wish to hold the bib (or tether) so they both feel safe and secure. After walking start to jog in a straight line.

- Consider which side they prefer standing on.

Activity 1

For speed

- Reinforce teaching points delivered by the teacher.

- Once confidence is achieved, allow both parties to experiment with speed over 10m.

- Practise responding to a starter.

- Set a distance and allow the pair to walk it first (if necessary). A peer or TA call out 'on your marks', 'set', 'go' and then sprint with the sighted person feeding back distances and guiding their partner.

Activity 2

For distance

- Consider encouraging turns (to mimic that of bends on a running track).

- Encourage communication between each runner.

- Try to give an example of scale as to how far they may be running and use guided discovery to assist with pace.

- Could walk first 100m, jog next, walk etc to build up partnership.

Teaching Assistant Card 8 (suggested for athletics)

Wheelchair drills for young people who may have difficulty walking or climbing stairs.

Learning Outcome: To develop sharp turning wheelchair skills

This card is designed to help young people that may have to develop their skills separately from the class with a peer, teaching assistant or in a small group. If several wheelchairs are available all students can participate and eventually compete against each other. If there is only one young person in a wheelchair consider developing their personal best times and technique.

Activity 1

- Start line (that are two cylinders about 1.22m apart), followed by one cylinder placed 1m away, then another cylinder 1m away, then another 1m away (3 in total and in a straight line).

Cylinders1m apart

Startline1.22m

Key Considerations

- Time the young person going in and around the cylinders (figure of 8).
- There is a 3 second infringement if the cylinder is touched and a 5 second infringement if the cylinder is knocked over.
- Widen cylinders if needed for greater success.
- Keep a record of times if young person responds to competition.

Teaching Points

- Look at positioning of hands to make sure a committed push is made.
- Encourage a pulling and pushing action in order to create tight turns.
- Consider sacrificing speed until technique is developed.
- Use body momentum to help push the wheelchair.
- Maintain a solid core to help with balance.

Teaching Assistant Card 9 (suggested for athletics)

Wheelchair drills for young people who may have difficulty walking or climbing stairs

Learning Outcome: To develop power, speed and turning skills

This card is designed to help young people that may have to develop their skills separately from the class with a peer, teaching assistant or within a small group. If several wheelchairs are available all students can participate and eventually compete against each other. If there is only one young person in a wheelchair consider developing their personal best times and technique.

Key Considerations

- The young person wheels over a safety mat and enters into a square indicated by 4 cylinders and measured by the dimensions 2.5m by 2.5m.

- They complete a 360° manoeuvre within the square and then wheels back over the mat, through the start/finish cylinders.

- 3 seconds infringement if a cylinder is touched. 5 seconds added if a cylinder is knocked over.

- 3 seconds added if they leave the square by the wrong line, 3 seconds added if a wheel passes over a line that is the perimeter of the square and 3 seconds added if the athlete does not complete the full length of the mat.

Activity 1

- Narrow the square if too easy, widen and shorten distance if too hard.

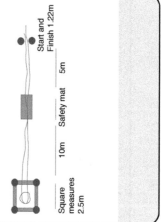

Square measures 2.5m

10m Safety mat 5m

Start and Finish 1.22m

Teaching points

- Encourage a strong start position, body forward, arms ready to push hard.

- A powerful drive to the mat, good momentum is needed. Look at arm position (is full range being used?)

- Look at hand placement, is it a full drive to the bottom of the wheel?

Teaching Assistant Card 10 (suggested for athletics)

Wheelchair drills for young people who may have difficulty walking or climbing stairs

Learning Outcome: To develop accuracy, agility and speed

This card is designed to help young people that may have to develop their skills separately from the class with a peer, teaching assistant or within a small group. If several wheelchairs are available all students can participate and eventually compete against each other. If there is only one young person in a wheelchair consider developing their personal best times and technique.

Key Considerations

- To complete 2 x 360° around two cylinders.

- 3 seconds will be added if a cylinder is touched and 5 seconds if they knock the cylinder over.

- The finish is when the last wheel touches the finish line.

- Keep a record of the time it takes to complete the task

Activity 1

- Set out the course, start line 1.22m in width. 5m to first cylinder, 5m to next. Set in a straight line.

- The young person must achieve 360° around each cylinder.

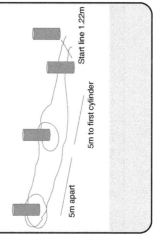
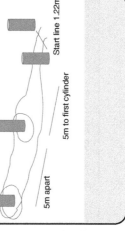

5m apart

5m to first cylinder

Start line 1.22m

Teaching Points

- Look at positioning of hands to make sure a committed push is made.

- Encourage a pulling and pushing action in order to create tight turns.

- Consider sacrificing speed until technique is developed.

- Use body momentum to help push the wheelchair.

Teaching Assistant Card 11 (suggested for athletics)

Wheelchair drills for young people who may have difficulty walking or climbing stairs.

Learning Outcome: To develop stamina, concentration and reversing skills

This card is designed to help young people that may have to develop their skills separately from the class with a peer, teaching assistant or within a small group. If several wheelchairs are available all students can participate and eventually compete against each other. If there is only one young person in a wheelchair consider developing their personal best times and technique.

Key Considerations

- The young person starts from behind the designated line, indicated by cylinders.
- The young person wheels over 2 mats placed slightly apart.
- The young person zig zag's around the cones, then reverses into the square (indicated by cylinders), manoeuvres 180° to leave from the opposite end of the square facing forwards.
- The young person zig zags back down the cones and goes back over the mats to the finish.
- 3 seconds infringement if a cone/cylinder is touched. 5 seconds added if a cylinder is knocked over.
- 3 seconds added if they leave the square by the wrong line, 3 seconds added if a wheel passes over the wrong line that is the perimeter of the square.

Activity 1

- The course can be flexible to suit the ability of the young person.
- Remove or add elements to provide suitable challenge.

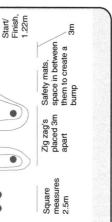

Square measures 2.5m

Zig zag's placed 3m apart

Safety mats, space in between them to create a bump 3m

Start/ Finish, 1.22m

Teaching Points

- Look at positioning of hands to make sure a committed push is made.
- Encourage speed to attack the mats.
- Encourage a pulling and pushing action in order to create tight turns.
- Consider sacrificing speed until technique is developed.
- Use body momentum to help push the wheelchair.
- Encourage looking over the shoulder when reversing.

Teaching Assistant Card 12 (suggested for athletics)

Wheelchair drills for young people who may have difficulty walking or climbing stairs

Learning Outcome: To develop explosive speed

This card is designed to help young people that may have to develop their skills separately from the class with a peer, teaching assistant or within a small group. If several wheelchairs are available all students can participate and eventually compete against each other. If there is only one young person in a wheelchair consider developing their personal best times and technique.

Key Considerations

- To complete the distance as fast as they can.
- The finish is when the last wheel touches the finish line.
- On 'go!' the young person wheels up to the set distance (20m, 30m etc).
- Keep a record of the time it takes to complete the sprint.

Activity 1

- Set out a start line and decide the distance to sprint to.
- The course can be flexible to suit the ability of the young person, change the distance, you can create a 'there and back' course if preferred.
- A flat surface would be ideal but areas with gradient, different terrain may help the development of skill and strength.

Teaching Points

- Look at positioning of hands to make sure a committed push is made.
- Encourage leaning forward to 'get behind the push'.
- Investigate if long pushes or short, quick pushes gain momentum more.
- If terrain is more challenging or has a gradient, then work at a slower rate before timings are suggested.

Teaching Assistant Card 13 (suggested for gymnastics)

Balancing for young people who may have difficulty walking or climbing stairs

Learning Outcome: To develop extension, tension and stillness

This card has been designed to assist the inclusion of young people who are in a wheelchair, or who need a frame to assist when walking. Reinforce the teaching points delivered by the teacher and always try to ask the young person what they want to achieve from the activity or how they can adapt it themselves.

Key Considerations

- Aim to be able to hold a balance for 5 seconds, unaided, if possible.

- Work from a secure and stable position (in chair or out, check this with teacher and young person).

- Focus on developing tension through body parts.

Activity 1

- Discuss centre of gravity and where theirs may be.

- Explore range of movement and practise holding shapes with arms;

- The young person can use props to help them balance (wall, hoop, bench).

- Consider using items to balance on their body to develop stillness and tension (bean bag, cone).

Activity 2

- Progress to partner or small group balances to encourage social interaction.

- Remind the young person to extend their limbs, sit tall, keep head straight, and have tension and stillness

Index

Note: *Italic* page numbers refer to *photos*.

Lightning Source UK Ltd.
Milton Keynes UK
UKHW052231281022
411293UK00004B/74